EDITED BY Kathy M. Collins and Darby M. Roberts

FOREWORD BY D. Stanley Carpenter

LEARNING IS NOT A SPRINT

Assessing and Documenting Student Leader Learning in Cocurricular Involvement

NASPA

Student Affairs Administrators
in Higher Education

Learning is Not a Sprint: Assessing and Documenting Student Leader Learning in Cocurricular Involvement

Published by
NASPA–Student Affairs Administrators in Higher Education
111 K Street, NE
10th Floor
Washington, DC 20002
www.naspa.org

Additional copies may be purchased by contacting the NASPA publications department at 301-638-1749 or visiting http://bookstore.naspa.org.

NASPA does not discriminate on the basis of race, color, national origin, religion, sex, age, gender identity, gender expression, affectional or sexual orientation, or disability in any of its policies, programs, and services.

Library of Congress Cataloging-in-Publication Data

Learning is not a sprint : assessing and documenting student leader learning in cocurricular involvement / edited by Kathy M. Collins and Darby M. Roberts ; foreword by D. Stanley Carpenter. -- 1st ed.
    p. cm.
 ISBN 978-0-931654-99-2
 1. Student affairs services--United States. 2. Experiential learning--United States. I. Collins, Kathy M. II. Roberts, Darby M.
 LB2342.9.L44 2012
 378.1'97--dc23
                    2012013103

Printed and bound in the United States of America
FIRST EDITION

CONTENTS

Appendices

FOREWORD

D. Stanley Carpenter

What do you remember from your college years? What were the insights that shaped you, and how did they come about? If you say that your top moment was the day you finally understood the Central Limit Theorem or any other purely academic concept, then you would be the only person I ever met to do so. For me, even the best classes or teachers were memorable more for their impact on my critical thinking skills, for raising the bar for my cognitive standards for analysis or detecting untruth, for learning an elegant new style of thinking and expression. In short, the subject matter, the information per se was not the crucial thing about my education. Rather, I was learning ways of thinking about and evaluating all the data around me. In constructivist terms, I was learning to create meaning, to make sense. In rationalist terms, I was organizing and classifying, figuring out cause and effect or the need for more data. And if the learning in formal classes was in some sense indirect, almost separate from the subject matter, the rest of my education was even more disconnected.

It is fashionable now for some to talk about the "other" education, the co(equal)-curriculum and its role in student learning. That is, it is fashionable for those of us in student affairs. For nearly all students, most faculty, and the vast majority of parents and politicians, this is nonsense. While they understand that students do change and grow emotionally and socially during college, they do not attribute the change to anything other than natural maturation and some vague notion about the college experience. The idea that students might be learning outside of class is frequently regarded with skepticism and is even a bit unsettling—who is directing this surreptitious learning and what are their goals? And yet, once students are taught what to look for with the guidance of student affairs professionals and helped to reflect, they are readily able to articulate all sorts of positive learning outcomes of student activities, peer-helping opportunities, residential programming, and the myriad other things promulgated by student affairs professionals. In fact, most involved students will express the belief that their out-of-class education is more important than classroom learning. While they usually experience their college years as a seamless experience, they understand intrinsically that their cognitive learning and their experiential learning are complementary, perhaps even synergistic. Such things as time management, conflict resolution, communication, problem solving, and decision making care little where they are learned. They pay dividends in many venues.

This book, then, is part of a larger and vital conversation about the learning that is attendant to involvement. We have known for some years that engagement in campus activities and with faculty in ways other than pedagogy have sizable impact on learning in a variety of forms and venues. However, we in student affairs have not figured out how to get that message out to faculty, to parents, to regulators, to accreditors, or even to students in a systematic and large-scale way. To be sure, there are pockets of excellence, institutional or divisional success stories, anecdotes that we all use to justify our existence. But there is no urgency across the board, no understanding that a good education requires not just a transfer of information or even prescribed experiences, but also an interaction with an educational, social, and emotional milieu in which the outcome(s) are undefined and even often in doubt or obscured. As budgets are tightened, divisions of student affairs are disbanded, and accreditors want to know about learning outcomes across the board, perhaps it is time to act.

How we go about intentionally fostering high-quality experiential learning that has both purpose and spontaneity for every student is more than a worthy topic, it has policy implications and social justice ramifications. As just one example, the first chapter of this book includes a marvelous discussion of the causes and prevalence of isomorphism in universities. This slavish imitation of one another by our best institutions works heavily against serving an increasingly diverse college student population, since the universities have never truly done so, and isomorphism implies an almost fatal inertia. The best and fastest remedy is to personalize the experiences of students by facilitating a wide range of activities that encourage involvement, engagement, and reflection. In this way, the student can largely create his or her own educational experience that draws upon the resources of the university without succumbing to the potential of the organization to crush individuality in the name of specious "standards." If we can do this right—if we can articulate the learning outcomes and provide assessment evidence that they are being met and are valid—we can help our universities get out of their own way.

Another policy issue that deserves mention is the notion that all higher education is somehow equal. Our massive focus on the cognitive, on subject matter, leads us to believe that for-profit exchange of money for information is the same as a residential college education. After all, both lead to the same degree. We also stand idly by and let purveyors of various kinds claim that all or nearly all students can benefit from online education, that education does not suffer if you work full time while attending, that professors are largely superfluous, not to mention expensive, especially the tenure track ones, and physical campuses are passé, simply waiting another decade or two to die. The antidote to all this tripe is a clearer understanding of out of class learning, the experiential component of college. Nontraditional and hybrid forms of learning can be effective and are the best option, sometimes the only option, in some cases. But we need to stop pretending that they are automatically or even by and large equivalent in quality to educational programs that include opportunities for planned and unplanned activities facilitated and evaluated by professionals, who intentionally apply theory and assess the results. If they really are equivalent, then student affairs would not and should not exist.

To summarize, it is time to act, intentionally, with an understanding of the state of the art in theory, in practice, and in assessment. And that is why this book is so timely and important. Rarely will one find in one tome the variety of perspectives from all levels of administration, from many different organizational venues, and from several different areas of the nation. There is also a good mix of theory and practice, with a clear understanding of how each informs the other. Anyone who reads this book should be able to discern a place to start supporting his or her organization in truly, intentionally helping students get more out of their educations by experiencing and reflecting. In addition, there is sufficient sophistication here to engage people who are not student affairs professionals, such as faculty or auxiliary professionals, in a dialogue about seamless educational experience, transfer learning, assessment, and many other crucial topics.

And that brings me to a final point. This book and others like it, along with relevant articles, reports, and internal and external studies, should be on the agenda of every student affairs division and department in the nation. We have to be able to articulate the reasons for our existence and our contributions to the educational enterprise in compelling and meaningful ways and to a variety of audiences. It is past time to get serious about this. Our survival as a field depends on it, but more importantly, the better we understand the mechanisms and impacts of out-of-class learning the better will be the educational experiences of students from all backgrounds. Such a worthy goal demands our best efforts.

CHAPTER 1

THE CURRENT STUDENT AFFAIRS AND HIGHER EDUCATION ENVIRONMENT

Where Are We Now?

Dean Bresciani

At perhaps no time in recent decades has student affairs been more central to a quality university experience and the learning environment therein. Yet we also face unprecedented economic challenges that are almost ubiquitous at national, state, and local levels. As a result, and in stark contrast to its centrality, student affairs as a profession and function within typical higher education settings is perhaps in more danger than ever before of being reduced, collapsed with other functions, or eliminated entirely. That is the admittedly subjective perspective of a student affairs career professional, but one who is now the president of a Carnegie Commission "Very High Research" land-grant university. Add to that, someone with graduate preparation in student affairs, balanced by doctoral degrees in higher education finance and in economics.

The paradox suggested above that faces student affairs calls for sober evaluation of the profession's maturation and development over recent decades, an evaluation that includes identifying and considering the circumstances in which student affairs makes a unique institutional contribution that requires specific educational and professional preparation.

Also, the profession needs to step back and candidly consider those situations in which student affairs provides a complementary and perhaps commendable but less than core institutional contribution. This scrutiny can be a challenge for student affairs professionals who, due to the passion and commitment to students' experiences that brought them into the profession, often find it challenging to step back from their work and evaluate their contributions in a detached and dispassionate manner.

Complicating the current environment is the fact that many if not most institutional presidents still come to their role through traditional academic channels of preparation. That circumstance is slowly but steadily shifting somewhat, or at least there is some broadening in paths of preparation. But for the time being, traditional paths to institutional leadership remain by far the most common, and those in such roles often have limited, if any, understanding of, much less appreciation for, the role and implications of a quality student affairs function or the extensive education, preparation, and expertise that student affairs practitioners bring to the college or university setting.

That being the case, institutional leaders will too often, but perhaps understandably, act without full appreciation of the substantive contributions of their institution's student affairs functions. In fact, newly appointed institutional senior leaders have recently reorganized or even eliminated student affairs portfolios. Ironically, those functions often have substantial implications for many of the key measures by which institutions and the success of their leaders are evaluated. Nonetheless, in the current environment, institutional leaders are often inclined to reduce, collapse, combine, or worse yet dismiss student affairs-associated expenses. They perceive them as easily recoverable expenses with few, if any, implications. Furthermore, when those leaders test their understandable but limited perspectives with academic and business affairs colleagues whose viewpoints are similarly limited, they find little argument to the contrary as they look for the "low-hanging fruit" to solve institutional resource challenges. At the same time, Kuh and Ikenberry (2009) concluded that institutions need to be better at assessing student learning, making decisions about resource allocation, and communicating actions to their various stakeholders. Student affairs staff can be key resources in that endeavor, but they have not historically been considered key to the academic environment.

It may be helpful for student affairs professionals to borrow from the historic and well-respected literature of organizational theory and behavior to further examine the challenges and solutions the profession faces in maintaining and enhancing the role of student affairs in increasing complex and competitive organizational environments.

Through a Different Lens

In the current economic environment and as perhaps never before in recent history, strategic student affairs professionals need to evaluate—and just as important, need to effectively articulate—the contributions of the profession and those in it. However, they need to do so not simply through their own eyes, but through objective measures and through the eyes of their colleagues within the colleges and universities in which they work and the eyes of the external constituencies they ultimately serve. Due to isomorphic tendencies common to the organization of higher education institutions, that evaluation needs to be done not simply on the level of a single institution but also in a collective sense as a profession.

Institutional leaders across the country increasingly seek to identify "non-core" functions and services. This is particularly true of those without a broad and comprehensive understanding of such programs and services. These campus leaders often look to common organizational structures and the increasingly common "organizational restructuring" of peer higher education institutions. This isomorphic tendency is not unique or unusual to higher education; in fact it has long been studied in both private and public organizational settings (e.g., DiMaggio & Powell, 1983; Fennell, 1980; Meyer, 1979).

Therefore, it is more important than ever for student affairs professionals to share and collaboratively consider their roles. More and more, the implications of reductions, if not eliminations, at one college or university will not be limited to that institution. In these economically desperate times, reorganizations at one institution may become a template for the leaders of other institutions to follow. To further understand these tendencies and the challenges the student affairs profession faces, it may be instructive to look at historic and well-established explanations of isomorphism and at concerns for what critics refer to as "administrative bloat" (Grassmuck, 1990, 1991) common to organizations that provide nonmaterial programs and services which, by their nature, are perceived as difficult if not impossible to quantify.

As outlined by Bresciani (1996), DiMaggio and Powell (1983) discussed two broad categories of isomorphism previously identified by Fennell (1980) and Meyer (1979). These categories seem particularly relevant to higher education settings: competitive isomorphism and institutional isomorphism. The definitions and delineations of these categories may overlap, depending on how they are operationalized, but the general concept of isomorphism can provide an important framework for this analysis.

Citing Hannan and Freeman (1977), DiMaggio and Powell (1983) presented competitive isomorphism as emphasizing market competition, niche change, and fitness measures. Although these features largely addressed organizational entry to and exit from capital markets, some aspects seem quite applicable—and even surprisingly familiar—to higher education institutions and a discussion of trends in the organization and delivery of student affairs functions.

Higher education institutions operate under a unique combination of incentives to maximize revenue and prestige, as well as "intra-" and "inter-" organizational competition. To maintain their competitive positions, higher education institutions must be attentive and sensitive to any new product "variations" introduced by competing institutions, as is typical in the classic oligopic market environment. Thompson (1989) described oligopic markets as "synonymous with competition among the few" (p. 330). The effect is that each institution has such a prominent market position that its behavior has direct repercussions on rival institutions. The interaction of organizations in oligopic competition is reflected in product price, sales volume, market share, differentiation, promotion, innovation, customer service, etc. It certainly can be argued that major research institutions are members of such a market environment, as are selective admission liberal arts institutions, and even mid-size regional institutions in geographic proximity.

As further discussed by Bresciani (1996), while competitive isomorphism may serve to explain initial innovations, it does not comprehensively address ongoing organizational behaviors. For this, DiMaggio and Powell (1983) turned to a discussion of institutional isomorphism as first suggested by Kanter (1972). Kanter depicted institutional isomorphism as taking one of three forms: coercive, mimetic, or normative.

Coercive processes, both formal and informal, result when pressure is applied to resource-dependent organizations by resource-controlling organizations. This can be as direct and obvious as the statistical reporting requirements of the federal government or as indirect and subtle as favorable treatment of an organization by special interest constituencies after a key issue between the two has been reconciled. Furthering the latter scenario, it has been argued, in resource allocation decisions, the political ramifications of administrators' actions may provide a far more powerful incentive than efficiency (Caruthers & Orwig, 1979; Covaleski & Dirsmith, 1988). Taking those perspectives a step further, the specific expectations placed on higher education institutions in general and student affairs functions specifically are felt most directly by those accountable to broadening constituencies. As institutional leaders attempt to meet the expectations of their operational area, associated expenditures naturally increase. "In order to survive, organizations conform to what is societally defined as appropriate and efficient, largely disregarding the actual impact on organizational performance" (Tolbert & Zucker, 1983, p. 26).

Echoing these coercive influences in a study of higher education institutions, Tolbert

(1985) defined resource dependency as the "environmental relations" between resource-subordinate organizations and their superordinate organizations. Studying the administrative structures of these institutions, Tolbert found a link between funding sources and, in segments lacking institutionalization, the creation of administrative units to address those sources. In this study and in previous research on the diffusion of civil service reform (Tolbert & Zucker, 1983), the intensity of the dependency was found to have a strong correlation with the institutionalization of superordinate organization structures. As that intensity or reliance increased, so did the rate of institutionalization of structures responding to the resources and structures of the superordinate organizations.

Another variation of institutional isomorphism involves mimetic processes, which result from uncertainty. Lacking sure technologies and systems, organizations imitate comparable (presumably successful) organizations that have a needed process or procedure already in place. The effects of this environmental uncertainty are significant in the decision-making processes of organizations (Leblebici & Salancik, 1981; Pfeffer, Salancik, & Leblebici, 1976). Imitating similar institution structures not only provides a ready solution to a given problem but also may help legitimize the solution to constituencies. Most higher education institutions are acutely aware of the funding, organization, and policies of peer institutions and commonly use those institutions to gauge the comparable features at their own institution.

A third variation of institutional isomorphism entails normative processes, which are encouraged by the increasing levels of bureaucratization, professionalization, and specialization in society and, more specifically, in higher education. Lacking established, rational structures, organizations legitimize their structures (indeed, their very existence) by adhering to the expected behaviors and structures established by dominant organizations and to the expectations shared by members of society (Zucker, 1977, 1982, 1983). As suggested by Tolbert (1985), Meyer and Rowan (1977, 1978), and DiMaggio and Powell (1983), organizations recognize pressures to adapt their structures and behaviors to accepted norms.

> When some organizational elements become institutionalized, that is, when they are widely understood to be appropriate and necessary components of the organization, organizations are under considerable pressure to incorporate these elements into their formal structure in order to maintain their legitimacy. (Tolbert & Zucker, 1983, p. 26)

This third variation of institutional isomorphism may be particularly applicable to present conditions in the maturing profession of student affairs.

The term "administrative bloat," as described by Bergman (1991), Halfond (1991), Andersen (1991), and Grassmuck (1990, 1991), may well support the normative perspective. Abundant organizational behavior literature suggests that the status of managers is closely associated with the size and importance of their responsibilities and the breadth and size of their subsequent budgets, staffs, and office divisions (Pfeffer, 1981; Salancik & Pfeffer, 1974; Whyte, 1957; Williamson, 1986). Other authors (Pondy, 1970; Williamson, 1970, 1986) have similarly proposed that promotion is implicitly introduced within closed hierarchical structures by increasing the number of subordinate members or levels. It could certainly be argued that administrators' proximity to and discretionary control of resource allocation processes empower them significantly toward such promotions (White, 1974).

Duplication of effort is also likely to increase as bureaucratic complexity and competition between administrators disenfranchise individuals from often poorly defined institutional missions, priorities, and control (Moch, 1976). Discretionary replication may not only be perpetuated, but may actually be encouraged through subtle competition among various subunits and the administrators responsible for those subunits. Individual administrators—particularly in those detached from academic "production" activities—may be inclined to view their own direct responsibilities as a first priority (Riggs, 1960). Tangentially, they may perceive these priorities as conveniently coinciding with those of their constituencies (Niskanen, 1971). Finally, and from perhaps a more sympathetic perspective, professional administrators may be altruistically inclined to improve both the quality and quantity of the services they provide.

The specialization or professionalization of management is indeed founded on the ideal of improvement and expansion of services. The goal of administrative specialization is defined as an attempt to respond more efficiently and rationally and to meet real needs. Along these lines, it can be defensively suggested that introducing and expanding services is the appropriate response to previously underserved needs. In other words, the future critical assessment of the growth of administration in higher education and, until recently, the burgeoning field of student affairs should not be based on past or even current administrative ratios.

Returning to the tendency for growth of administrative and student affairs versus core academic expenditures, the general concept of isomorphism may now prove useful in explaining the disparate contemporary trends. It seems unlikely that isomorphic influences would add significantly to expenditures for the academic activities of higher education institutions. Most reasonably comparable institutions have for some time structured themselves similarly and pursued extremely similar instructional, research, and service activities. In addition, a certain mystique surrounding the process of education substantially shields the field of academics from external influence or control. Whether isomorphism acts to define or reproduce expectations, its effect is obvious in the similar structural characteristics of academic and, increasingly, of service offerings among like and even dissimilar higher education institutions. Again, as more diverse segments of society enter public higher education, contemporary service and support expenditures are likely to increase, and indeed have increased until recently.

Bresciani (1996) suggested an analytical tool that may help to apply the concepts of isomorphism and professionalization to higher education—a tool of discretionary versus deterministic management behavior (Pondy, 1969; Williamson, 1964, 1970, 1986). Although the original perspective was developed in the context of a private firm, its applicability to higher education is appealing. As Pondy noted, in the classic owner-manager firm, organizational structures and management decisions are profit motivated. The allocation of resources is technologically determined: Marginal costs must equal marginal benefits. In traditional economic theory, expenditures for administration must be similarly motivated. However, the separation of ownership from control dramatically alters that calculus (Berle, 1959). In nonowner-manager organizations, the profit motive may be sublimated to what Williamson (1967, 1970, 1986) described in detail as the utility function or incentive distraction of the professional manager. This utility function is loosely defined by the manager's autonomy, workload, authority, or hierarchical position within the organization. "Opportunity sets" (Williamson, 1970) become available to the nonowner-manager, who may choose to allocate resources in ways that will realize acceptable profits (organizational success) but, more importantly, will serve his or her personal utility in an "expense-preference" manner. The dichotomy between deterministic and discretionary decisions may be particularly powerful in evaluating the allocation environments and decisions suggested by the above three perspectives. The classic 1932 Berle and Means query, "Have we any justification for assuming that those in control of the modern corporation will choose to operate it in the interests of the shareholders?" rings an ominous note when applied to higher education. Higher education today, as is well appreciated, no longer enjoys exception to that concern and in fact has become an easy target for critics.

While the treatises on organizational theory and behavior highlighted above are historical classics in that field, their application to the contemporary challenges of higher education may be powerful. That being the case, thoughtful student affairs professionals will focus efforts to define their role not just for their own setting, but more broadly across the profession and as a distinguishable and value-added function rather than a redundant and thus dispensable one. Of course, that is easier said than done, particularly given the broad-ranging and often divergent preparation, demands, and priorities of practitioners in student affairs arenas. In no other aspect of higher education is there more complexity to the preparation and expertise of faculty and staff, nor more dynamic demands on them, than in the student affairs profession. Nonetheless, student affairs professionals need not only to define their expertise and contributions but also to differentiate them from the expertise and contributions of others in the academy. Failure to do so will give rise to questions of redundancy with academic and other colleagues, an argument in which student affairs is rarely positioned to prevail.

Ewell (2009) summarized four major changes in the higher education assessment movement in the past 20 years that have also had an impact on student affairs. The first, perceived legitimacy, indicates that more academics than ever before accept the need for assessment to provide evidence of student success to external stakeholders such as accreditors. Ewell's second change, the new policy centrality of higher education, addresses the urgency of educating our citizens to be competitive in a global economy. Along with that urgency comes the responsibility to be transparent and proactive in developing and assessing learning outcomes. Ewell's third change is that external stimuli for higher education are now accreditors rather than states. In the past, states took a more proactive role in accountability and funding, but when regional accrediting agencies grew in stature, states were able to shift focus. Accreditors have been able to promote both accountability and improvement. Finally, Ewell's fourth change is the importance in recent years of assessment technology as a means to measure the effectiveness of higher education. The resources available now, such as task-based assessments, electronic portfolios, and national surveys, far exceed what we had a few short years ago. Ewell concluded that the contradiction between accountability and improvement has lessened. "[B]ecause the stakes associated with higher education are so much higher for policy makers today, aggressive action on the accountability agenda is more likely and a proactive response on the part of the academy is more urgent" (p. 7). These issues will be explored in more detail in later chapters.

In the past two decades, the profession's focus on student learning and on its measurement has increasingly become the priority and vernacular of the student affairs profession. In a functional sense, that has been commendable and productive. Student affairs practitioners have increasingly come to think of themselves—and indeed take an active role— as educators. In many settings, they very arguably fill that role in a broad-definition sense of the term. However, in the current economic environment, that role has not been without liabilities in terms of institutional politics. It could also be argued that their self-definition positions them to be compared and conflicted with academic colleagues, who traditionally have defined themselves similarly, if not uniquely, in that manner. Such a conundrum can lead to understandable concerns about redundancy of roles, which while rarely, if ever, is quite the case in practice, is still a perception and question that puts student affairs professionals in a difficult if not risky institutional position.

(Re)defining the Student Affairs Profession

The profession needs to better articulate the unique roles and expertise it provides. The strategic orientation for doing this should not be through the profession's eyes but through the eyes of internal and external higher education colleagues, consumers, and constituents.

A counterintuitive approach for articulating the profession's functions might be a "reverse hypothesis" approach: What would *not* be done or realized in higher education settings without the skills and contributions uniquely provided by student affairs professionals? In other words, what expertise and contributions do academic, business affairs, and other colleagues *not* provide? Furthermore, what skills and contributions do those colleagues lack the capacity to provide?

Articulating those contributions that only student affairs professionals are uniquely prepared to provide would perhaps be a first step in better positioning the broader roles and responsibilities of student affairs functions. Describing student affairs activities not simply as complementing, extending, or competing with the skills and contributions of academic and business affairs colleagues but rather as unique contributions from the field and practice of student affairs would serve to more productively differentiate and insulate student affairs from concerns for redundancy and elevate the at-times irreplaceable nature of the field's contributions.

Let us not forget that the expectations and responsibilities placed on higher education institutions, particularly those in the public sector (which increasingly involves all institutions regardless of public or private basis), have become more complex and dynamic than ever before, and they extend well beyond a narrow focus on scholarly achievement. It goes without saying that higher education, both in terms of access to it and success within it, has become a virtually obligatory key to social mobility. The move from mass demand to a universal demand for higher education, highlighted some 40 years ago by Trow (1970), has been a long-developing and well-documented trend, both in terms of the demand for higher education and the complexity of issues surrounding that demand. While this trend is not new, it is still nonetheless perhaps not commonly understood by discipline-specific scholars and the individuals traditionally emerging from those ranks to institutional leadership positions. At best, this lack of understanding creates a challenging balancing act between increasingly reduced institutional resources and increasingly greater demands for them.

Hard Questions

What is the contemporary role of student affairs in higher education settings, or more specifically, what should it be? It is clear that the general obligation of student affairs is the enhancement of student access, support, and out-of-class activities—and their leading to retention and graduation success. As illustrated in Chapters 2 and 3, the breadth of scholarship is well established on the importance of student's activities outside of the classroom as a critical cognate of their success, postsecondary graduation, and success beyond graduation. Yet the contributions of those creating and organizing those experiences remain poorly defined and often unappreciated. It can be argued that the profession needs to ask itself why.

Why, as a common solution to reducing expenditures on student affairs programs and services, are these functions reorganized under other areas, eliminated, or outsourced to the private sector? Why are the limitations and liabilities of doing so, from an educational perspective, rarely appreciated or considered? Put another way, why are the preparation and contributions of the student affairs professional so often dismissed? Is it because we have too long focused on what is important to us as individuals and as a profession rather than what is important and prioritized by our institutions?

Have student affairs professionals engaged in those institutional needs and demands and developed the skill sets requisite to executing them at the highest standards? Or has the profession become defensive of what its practitioners enjoy doing, at the expense of doing what needs to be done and developing new and dynamic skills to meet those demands?

In some respects, it could be argued that student affairs has had more foresight of and been more responsive to the dynamic changes in higher education than any other section of the academy. For decades, graduate preparation programs have been increasing the focus on measurable learning outcomes, quantifying the "value added" from higher education experiences, and evaluating and accommodating the factors that lead to successful matriculation, retention, and graduation from postsecondary environments. That has often taken place in environments that were less than welcoming and encouraging but are not now pressed—if not comprehensively expected through increasing federal, state, and even local levels of public oversight and observation—to demonstrate those efforts and outcomes.

From a more critical perspective, however, has the profession focused on developmental outcomes at the expense of—or perhaps simply in benign indifference to—more material factors and their measurement? Similarly, has the profession and its graduate preparation programs adequately addressed and refined the professional preparation and expertise of student affairs professionals overseeing increasingly complex business and operational concerns? Many of those concerns feature capital and budgetary responsibilities of a scope and nature equal to if not exceeding those of any other aspect of the institution. Yet it would be difficult to argue that most student affairs practitioners have the same preparation in those financial fields as do their counterparts with similar responsibilities across the institution.

In an environment of accountability, not just for learning outcomes and educational value added but also for transparency, efficiency, and return on investment for operational concerns, can student affairs professionals responsible for such functions defend themselves as uniquely and better qualified to carry them out than others in their institutions? In some cases, the answer may be yes, but in others, the answer may put their roles in a perilous position. That is not to say that student affairs practitioners lend only limited value or no value compared to their institutional counterparts. In fact, the contrary is true. Nonetheless, are those qualities lost in the perception that institutional colleagues have superior preparation and that student affairs professionals are therefore redundant?

Developmental and even learning outcomes still remain too vague an aspect of a higher education experience, yet they have and will continue to be critical to its definition and success. But the unique combined skill set that student affairs practitioners bring to educational environments risk being eliminated in the competitive resource environment if those practitioners lack complementary and clear expertise in operational responsibilities. The following chapters offer a premise and definition of the potential to reposition the profession as a truly core aspect of the redefined "new normal" (Angel & Connelly, 2011; Ladd, 2011; Doyle & Delaney, 2009; Lumina Foundation for Education, 2010) of a quality higher education experience.

Questions for Reflection

1. What is the definition of student affairs in the contemporary context and in the context in which it will exist in the future? That is not a question of where it has come from or what student affairs professionals would wish the answer to be, but rather an encouragement to step back and consider the profession's part in the broader construct of future higher education settings.

2. What role does student affairs need to have in defining itself as a critical part of student success both outside and in the classroom through student engagement, and subsequently, retention and graduation? What objective measures can demonstrate that contribution, and what roles will the profession play in bringing those measures to the forefront?

3. As Kuh and Ikenberry (2009) posited:

   How can higher education reduce expenditures, maintain the gains achieved in access, improve graduation rates, and remain affordable while at the same time ensure that students acquire the skills, competencies, and dispositions that prepare them for a lifetime of learning in an increasingly competitive global marketplace? (p. 5)

References

Andersen, K. E. (1991, November/December). Anatomizing bloat. *Academe*, 20–24.

Angel, D., & Connelly, T. (2011). *Riptide: The new normal for higher education.* Ashland, KY: The Publishing Place.

Bergman, B. R. (1991, November/December). Bloated administration, blighted campuses. *Academe*, 12–16.

Berle, A. A., Jr. (1959). *Power without property.* New York, NY: Harcourt, Brace & Company.

Berle, A. A., Jr., & Means, G. C. (1932). *The modern corporation and private property.* New York, NY: Commerce Clearinghouse.

Bresciani, D. (1996). *Explaining administrative costs: A case study* (Doctoral dissertation, University of Arizona, 1996). UMI Dissertation Service, 9713408.

Caruthers, J. K., & Orwig, M. (1979). *Budgeting in higher education.* ERIC Clearinghouse on Higher Education (Report No. 3). Washington, DC: American Association for Higher Education.

Covaleski, M. A., & Dirsmith, M. W. (1988). An institutional perspective on the rise, social transformation, and fall of a university budget category. *Administrative Science Quarterly, 33*, 562–587.

DiMaggio, P. J., & Powell, W. W. (1983). The iron cage revisited: Institutional isomorphism and collective rationality in organizational fields. *American Sociological Review, 48*, 147–159.

Doyle, W. R., & Delaney J. A. (2009, July-August). Higher education funding: The new normal. *Change, 41*(4), pp. 60–62.

Ewell, P. (2009, November). *Assessment, accountability, and improvement: Revisiting the tension.* (NILOA Occasional Paper No.1). Urbana, IL: University of Illinois and Indiana University, National Institute for Learning Outcomes Assessment.

Fennell, M. L. (1980). The effects of environmental characteristics on the structure of hospital clusters. *Administrative Science Quarterly, 25*, 484–510.

Grassmuck, K. (1990, March 28). Big increases in academic-support staffs prompt growing concerns on campuses. *The Chronicle of Higher Education*, pp. A1, A32, A33, A35.

Grassmuck, K. (1991, August 14). Throughout the 80s, colleges hired more non-teaching staff than other employees. *The Chronicle of Higher Education*, p. A22.

Halfond, J. A. (1991, November/December). How to control administrative cost. *Academe*, 17–19.

Hannan, M. T., & Freeman, J. H. (1977). The population ecology of organizations. *American Journal of Sociology, 82*, 929–964.

Kanter, R. M. (1972). *Commitment and community*. Cambridge, MA: Harvard University Press.

Kuh, G., & Ikenberry, S. (2009). *More than you think, less than we need: Learning outcomes assessment in American higher education*. Urbana, IL: University of Illinois and Indiana University, National Institute for Learning Outcomes Assessment.

Ladd, H. (2011). *The new normal in U.S. postsecondary education*. Retrieved from The Parthenon Group website: http://www.parthenon.com/ThoughtLeadership/TheNewNormalinUSPostsecondaryEducation

Leblebici, H., & Salancik, G. (1981). Effects of environmental uncertainty on information and decision processes in banks. *Administrative Science Quarterly, 26*, 578–596.

Lumina Foundation for Education. (2010). *Navigating the "new normal."* Retrieved from http://www.luminafoundation.org/publications/Navigating_the_new_normal.pdf

Meyer, J. W. (1979). *The impact of the centralization of educational funding and control on state and local organizational governance* (Program Report No. 79-120). Stanford, CA: Institute for Research on Educational Finance and Governance, Stanford University.

Meyer, J. W., & Rowan, B. (1977). Institutional organizations: Formal structure as myth and ceremony. *American Journal of Sociology, 83*, 440–463.

Meyer, J. W., & Rowan, B. (1978). The structure of educational organization. In M. Meyer (Ed.), *Environments and organizations* (pp. 78–109). San Francisco, CA: Jossey-Bass.

Moch, M. K. (1976). Structure and organizational resource allocation. *Administrative Science Quarterly, 21*, 661–674.

Niskanen, W. (1971). *Bureaucracy and representative government*. Chicago, IL: Aldine.

Pfeffer, J. (1981). *Power in organizations*. Marshfield, England: Pitman.

Pfeffer, J., Salancik, G., & Leblebici, H. (1976). The effects of uncertainty on the use of social influence in organizational decision making. *Administrative Science Quarterly, 21*, 227–245.

Pondy, L. R. (1969). Effects of size, complexity, and ownership on administrative intensity. *Administrative Science Quarterly, 14*, 47–60.

Pondy, L. R. (1970). Toward a theory of internal resource allocation. In M. N. Zald (Ed.), *Power in organizations* (pp. 270–311). Nashville, TN: Vanderbilt University Press.

Riggs, F. W. (1960). Prismatic society and financial administration. *Administrative Science Quarterly, 5*, 1–46.

Salancik, G. R., & Pfeffer, J. (1974). The bases and use of power in organizational decision making: The case of a university. *Administrative Science Quarterly, 19*(4), 453–473.

Thompson, A. A., Jr. (1989). *Economics of the firm: Theory and practice*. Englewood Cliffs, NJ: Prentice Hall.

Tolbert, P. S. (1985). Institutional environments and resource dependency: Sources of administrative structure in institutions of higher education. *Administrative Science Quarterly, 30*, 1–13.

Tolbert, P. S., & Zucker, L. G. (1983). Institutional sources of change in the formal structure of organizations: The diffusion of civil service reform, 1880–1935. *Administrative Science Quarterly, 28*, 22–39.

Trow, M. (1970, Winter). Reflections on the transition from mass to universal higher education. *Daedalus, 99*(1), pp. 1–42.

White, P. E. (1974). Resources as determinants of organizational behavior. *Administrative Science Quarterly, 19*, 366–379.

Whyte, W. H. (1957). *The organization man*. Garden City, NJ: Doubleday Anchor.

Williamson, O. E. (1964). *The economics of discretionary behavior: Managerial objectives in a theory of the firm*. Englewood Cliffs, NJ: Prentice Hall.

Williamson, O. E. (1967). Hierarchical control and optimum firm size. *The Journal of Political Economy, 75*, 123–138.

Williamson, O. E. (1970). *Corporate control and business behavior: An inquiry into the effects of organization form on enterprise behavior.* Englewood Cliffs, NJ: Prentice Hall.

Williamson, O. E. (1986). *Economic organization: Firms, markets and policy control.* Sussex, England: Wheatsheaf.

Zucker, L. G. (1977). The role of institutionalization in cultural persistence. *American Sociological Review, 42,* 726–743.

Zucker, L. G. (1982). Institutional structure and organizational processes: The role of evaluation units in schools. In A. Bank, & R. C. Williams (Eds.), *Studies in evaluation and decision making* (pp. 69–89). (CSE Monograph Series in Evaluation, No. 10). Los Angeles, CA: Center for the Study of Evaluation.

Zucker, L. G. (1983). Organizations as institutions. In S. B. Bacharach (Ed.), *Perspectives in organizational sociology: Theory and research* (pp. 1–47). (ASA Series, Vol. 2). Greenwich, CT: JAI.

CHAPTER 2

LEADERSHIP AND STUDENT LEARNING
Where Do We Come From?

Sharra Durham Hynes

From the time of our birth, developmental milestones and achievements are tracked and documented by our physician, our parents, and our teachers to ensure that we are keeping up with expected growth and development (Kientz et al., 2007). From mastery of grasping objects as an infant to learning the alphabet as a preschooler, basic mathematical computations in elementary school, and more complex scientific equations in high school, our learning becomes intimately tied to our identity. In the college environment, learning and how we learn are also tied to our identity and our achievement of developmental milestones.

The study of learning and the assessment of teaching strategies have attracted significant interest within the last several decades, particularly in the United States, as we find ourselves slipping in academic performance and achievement compared to other nations (Sykes, 1995).

> Students from Birmingham and Boston no longer compete against each other for jobs; instead, their rivals are well-educated students from Sydney and Singapore. But as globalization has progressed, American educational progress

has stagnated. Today, the United States' high school graduation rate ranks near the bottom among developed nations belonging to the Organization for Economic Co-operation and Development (OECD). And on virtually every international assessment of academic proficiency, American secondary school students' performance varies from mediocre to poor. Given that human capital is a prerequisite for success in the global economy, U.S. economic competitiveness is unsustainable with poorly prepared students feeding into the workforce. (Alliance for Excellent Education Fact Sheet, 2008)

In part due to the aforementioned slip in academic performance, and also because of an ongoing interest in the science of learning, there have been numerous studies conducted and models put forth to explain the learning process and give suggestions for improvement. Scholars and researchers desiring to know how to aid individuals in the learning process have sought to determine how people best learn and how to accelerate or optimize the learning process (Mashek & Hammer, 2011). A line of research and practice has emerged called the Scholarship of Teaching and Learning (SoTL). SoTL occurs when there is systematic and purposeful reflection on the teaching and learning process (Mashek & Hammer, 2011).

While the emphasis on teaching and learning has been growing worldwide, the United States has seen a corresponding paradigm shift in higher education institutions. Described below, this paradigm shift has set up an opportunity for learning to be assessed and understood through both in-class and out-of-class experiences.

A paradigm shift is taking hold in American higher education. In its briefest form, the paradigm that has governed our colleges is this: A college is an institution that exists to provide instruction. Subtly but profoundly we are shifting to a new paradigm: A college is an institution that exists to produce learning. This shift changes everything. (DeZure, 2000, p. 198)

Another shift is the acknowledgement that learning takes place in contexts and environments other than the traditional classroom setting. Some authors have even expanded the definition of learning to include out-of-class learning.

We no longer believe that learning is the passive corollary of teaching, or that students do, or should, simply absorb material presented in lectures and textbooks. The new concept of *learning* recognizes the essential integration of personal development with learning; it reflects the diverse ways through which students may engage, as whole people with multiple dimensions and unique personal histories, with the tasks and content of learning. (Keeling, 2004, p. 3)

According to Keeling, this integrated learning helps to bridge the gap that has historically existed between academic learning and student development.

Simultaneous to the increased interest in how we learn has been a proliferation of writing on the topic of leadership development, both within higher education and in other contexts. Some writers have even referred to this proliferation as a growth industry. In an article on leadership development, Allio (2005) pointed out that a Google search for "leadership programs" yielded more than seven million matches. "Despite the abundance of writing on this topic, leadership has presented a major challenge to practitioners and researchers interested in understanding the nature of leadership. It is a highly valued phenomenon that is very complex" (Northouse, 2004, p. 10).

> Aligning with the growing interest in leadership and learning is the realization that we need better leaders who are equipped and ready to address the needs of our complex and changing world. The American public perceives a crisis of leadership in our nation. Major public and private institutions appear increasingly incapable of dealing constructively with an ever-expanding list of social and economic problems, and individuals are becoming more cynical about government. We need a new generation of leaders who can bring about positive change in local, national, and international affairs. (Zimmerman-Oster & Burkhardt, 1999, p. 5)

Case Study

The following case study highlights a situation where knowledge of student development theory, leadership theory, and learning theories would be instrumental in working with an individual student. While this situation is fictional, readers of this chapter will most likely be able to identify a student situation that parallels some dimension of the situation. The case is intended to apply the rich depth of theory that informs our work. The Social Change Model of Leadership Development is specifically referenced throughout the case. This model is explained in detail later in the chapter.

Mitchell, a sophomore studying business administration at a faith-based liberal arts institution, has just been elected sophomore class president. Mitch's college of 5,000 students is huge compared to his high school where the total enrollment was 400. The college is located in a suburb of a major metropolitan area, and service to others (both local and global) is a major theme for the institution.

Mitch comes from a small, rural town in the Midwest and had extensive leadership experience at his high school. He was a student who did everything—sports, music, drama, community service, church involvement, etc.—so it was natural for him to think about running for a leadership role at his college. He loves the limelight that leadership brings, and having others look up to him is a great feeling for him. He did well during his first year as a student at the college, and a group of his friends encouraged him to run for class president.

Mitch desires to get his MBA someday and wants to start a business that will be based in his small town—something that will provide jobs for those who have not taken the initiative to get an education but who still have skills and talents that can be developed. Mitch is an idealist and a perfectionist. He has high goals for himself and also places high expectations on others—peers, family members, coworkers, etc.

Mitch is elected by his peers to serve as their class president, and during the first week in his position, Mitch sits down with his class advisor. The advisor asks him what his goals are for the year. Mitch immediately begins to fidget in his chair. He is uneasy and he appears to draw a blank on goals and a vision for the year. When the advisor "digs in" a bit more, he tells her that he ran for the position because he wanted leadership experience on his résumé, he likes the feeling of being a leader, and he realized that he would win because no one else was running. The advisor then asks how he wants his team members, the other class officers, to work together this year. Again, he draws a blank. Mitch admits that he really does not have any ideas about developing his team or how they should work together. He says that he will pick up the slack for anyone who does not do his or her job. This is the way that he has always approached leadership before. Especially as the president, he knows that he is ultimately responsible for what does or does not get done.

The advisor rolls up her sleeves and begins to guide Mitch through the process of how he can craft a vision for the year ahead with his team members. She encourages Mitch to look at this as a year of learning and to take time to reflect on his experiences. She also encourages Mitch to identify a mentor, someone at the college whom he admires and desires to emulate. She recommends that Mitch meet regularly with this person to develop his leadership capabilities. Finally, the advisor and Mitch set some expectations for their relationship and commit to sharing openly with each other throughout the year.

When Mitch leaves the office, the advisor is keenly aware of the work that is ahead, and she begins to formulate an advising plan for working with Mitch. He has been oriented to the seven values of the Social Change Model of Leadership Development in his leadership class. The advisor reflects on the multiple models and theories about leadership and learning. How should she evaluate what Mitch believes about the seven values of the Social Change Model of Leadership Development and what his practice has been regarding behaviors associated with each of the values? What stage of the Leadership Identity Development Model might be assumed, based on what the advisor has learned about Mitch? Remember that he does not have a clear understanding of how a team can work together to achieve a goal or how interdependent team members may need to work together to get things done. Perhaps you are unable to answer these questions right now. Please read on for full explanations of the Social Change Model of Leadership Development and Leadership Identity Development Model. You will be more equipped to advise Mitch when you understand these models.

Leadership Theories and Student Learning

It is particularly important for higher education scholars and practitioners to integrate timely and relevant concepts of student learning with a clear understanding of leadership development within the college environment. This integration can be one step in building a generative learning environment (Mitchell, 2006). Generative learning shifts emphasis of the learning environment from being authority driven to being learner driven. It also assumes that educators will no longer simply provide answers to students but will teach them how to ask the appropriate questions to inform their learning process. Finally, a generative learning environment develops leadership within students and shares authority with them. Certainly this type of learning environment is not easy to develop. It requires intentional work and perhaps a paradigm shift for educators who are accustomed to operating in an instructional paradigm where teachers simply tell students what they need to know.

Two recent and relevant models of leadership development seem to be most appropriate and accessible for examining the integration of student learning with student leadership development. The Social Change Model of Leadership Development and the Leadership Identity Development Model were both developed with the college student experience and development processes in mind. It is also useful to understand the influences of other postindustrial views of leadership that are not tailored to the college student population or experience. These include, but are not limited to, transformational, relational, and adaptive leadership.

The Social Change Model of Leadership Development (SCM) was developed by a team of leadership scholars and was first published by the Higher Education Research Institute (HERI) in 1996. This model promotes leadership as a process that is filled with purpose and is grounded by a set of clearly identified shared values (HERI, 1996). As Komives and Wagner explained in the text *Leadership for a Better World* (2009), there are two primary goals of the model: to enhance student learning and development and to facilitate positive social change. The seven values that combine to create the synergy of positive change are citizenship, collaboration, common purpose, controversy with civility, consciousness of self, congruence, and commitment (Komives & Wagner, 2009). These values must blend and be operational in order to achieve the overarching value of change.

To fully understand the model, it is important to consider the definitions and associated constructs of each of the eight values. There are three personal values. The first is consciousness of self. As with many other leadership theories, this model begins with a baseline understanding of self. Specifically, the definition of this value is an "awareness of the values, emotions, attitudes, and beliefs that motivate one to take action" (Astin, 1996, p. 6). This awareness allows the individual to be an observer of his or her self in relationship to others. This concept is similar to what Heifetz described in his definition of adaptive leadership that involves movement between the dance floor and the balcony (Parks, 2005). Heifetz explained this phenomenon as leaders moving out of the day-to-day minutia in order to move to the balcony to gain some perspective on what is really happening in the organization. The balcony is referenced as the place to gain perspective; leaders are admonished to move back to the dance floor in order to implement any necessary changes.

Congruence, the second personal value, is the amount of consistency in one's thinking, feeling, behaving, and living. People who live with the value of congruence are able to live with authenticity and honesty toward others on a consistent basis (Astin, 1996). The last personal value is commitment. This value measures one's intensity and duration of action in relation to another person, idea, or activity. Astin (1996) described commitment as the source of energy for individual and collective efforts.

In addition to the personal values, the SCM contains three group values: collaboration, common purpose, and controversy with civility. Collaboration is characterized by an increase in a group's effectiveness because the group is able to tap into and maximize the individual talents of each group member to create the best possible outcome for a task or given project. The group benefits because the individual efforts create an outcome where the whole is greater than the sum of the individual parts. The second group value, common purpose, means that people work toward a shared set of aims and values. These shared values may be implicit or covertly stated within the group. "Common purpose is best achieved when all members of the group build and share in articulating the purpose and goals of the group work" (Astin, 1996, p. 6). The final group value is controversy with civility and is perhaps one of the most important and hard-to-achieve values when seeking to accomplish social change. This value delineates two fundamental realities. The first reality is that differences are inherent when working in any kind of group or even when working with one other person. The second reality is that, when these differences arise, they must be handled in the most open, respectful, and gracious way possible (Astin, 1996).

Finally, the SCM contains two community values: citizenship and change. Some may believe that the ultimate aim of the model is citizenship, but the other values should not be lost by placing importance solely on citizenship. Citizenship is defined as the "process whereby the self is responsibly connected to the environment and the community" (Astin, 1996, p. 7). This definition also implies active engagement in the group and in the community in order to serve these constituencies and to create lasting change. Change, the collective value that is implicitly connected to all the other values, is defined as the ability to maintain core functions of a group while simultaneously managing the complexities of a change effort. "The dynamic interaction across levels and between values contributes to social change for the common good, the eighth critical value associated with this model" (Dugan, 2006b, p. 336).

"Responsible citizenship and positive change are most likely to occur when the leadership group functions collaboratively with a common purpose and encourages civility in the expression of controversy" (Astin, 1996, p. 6). In this statement alone, one can clearly see the interrelationship of the values and the way in which the change value embodies the collective interaction of all of the other values. Although positive change is the ultimate outcome desired, benefits will be seen at the individual, society, or community level, and at the group level. See Figure 1 for a visual image of the interaction in and between the seven values.

Figure I
Social Change Model of Leadership Development (2011)

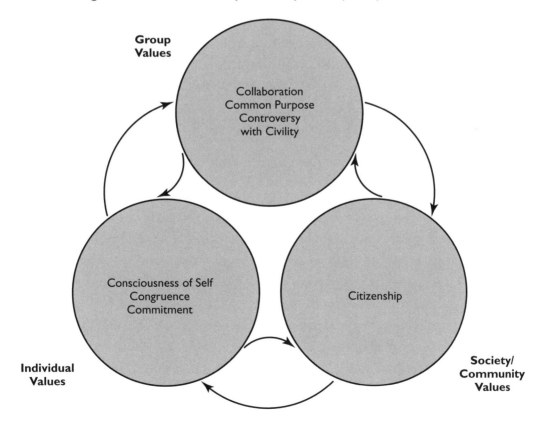

Those who created the SCM said, "We regard a leader as one who is able to effect positive change for the betterment of others, the community, and society. All people, in other words, are potential leaders" (HERI, 1996, p. 16). Acknowledging that all people can be leaders and that all people can become effective learners, we can firmly stand behind educational reform that calls for students to move beyond accumulating course credits and to gain knowledge and experience that builds real-world capabilities (Association of American Colleges and Universities [AAC&U], 2007). These real-world capabilities can begin to address insurmountable challenges in order to create meaningful, tangible, enduring, positive change.

In 2004, a team of researchers from the University of Maryland including Komives, Casper, Longerbeam, Mainella, and Osteen (2005), identified the Leadership Identity Development Model (LID), a grounded theory for developing a leadership identity. Grounded theories present an early analytic scheme from which additional research can be based (Denzin & Lincoln, 2003). The grounded theory of developing a leadership identity showed a developmental process of how students place themselves in the construct of leadership over time. From this grounded theory, a six-stage model of leadership identity development was created. The six stages are awareness, exploration/engagement, leader identified, leadership differentiated, generativity, and internalization/synthesis. In stage one, individuals are focused on others; they are seeking affirmation, and they do not understand that they have the capacity to be a person of influence. Stage two, exploration/engagement, involves the development of personal skills and abilities and building confidence in self. This stage is also marked by wanting to make a difference. In stage three, leader identified, the involvement in activities is narrowed to include activities that are personally meaningful. People begin to believe that leaders are the ones who can make things happen or get things done. In stage four, leadership differentiated, students have progressed through the key transition. Individuals are now able to see that one can lead from anywhere within an organization, not just as the positional leader. Stage five, generativity, includes the acknowledgement that leadership is a process. Individuals are now aware of the importance of teams and mentors. Finally, in stage six, internalization/synthesis, individuals are seeking to develop leadership in others and are adept at sharing responsibilities. They are also focused on the sustainability of organizations, not just on the present.

A deeper examination of the six stages reveals one common theme: the role that "others" play in developing both an individual's leadership identity as well as the role that "others" play in influencing a group's development. Peers and particularly older mentors are powerful influences, especially in stages three and four of the model. This emphasis on peers and older mentors can also be found in literature on transformative learning, or learning that intends to move individuals beyond tacit assumptions and expectations and toward meaning making and integration (Mezirow, 2000). "The concept of transformative learning and the distinct mode of meaning making it entails are grounded in the constructive-developmental perspective advanced most notably by Jean Piaget (1950)" (Hodge, Baxter Magolda, & Haynes, 2009, p. 3).

Another overlap between LID and transformative learning theory is the process of identifying new ways of knowing or constructing new ways of making meaning. These same principles align nicely with self-authorship, which is explored more fully in a later portion of this chapter and again in Chapter 7.

Finally, LID explains a key transition that occurs between stages three and four of the model, when students experience a shift in consciousness. They move from being independent to being interdependent. Once through this transition, they can say with confidence that leadership is not purely positional or about having authority over others. In stages four, five, and six, leadership can be found anywhere within a group of people who are trying to accomplish a task or achieve a goal. There is also acknowledgement in these higher stages that leaders are interdependent and need others in order to get things done.

In a qualitative study conducted by Durham Hynes at Texas A&M University in 2007, the LID model was used to examine a group of 10 students to learn more about the process whereby students at the university were coming to an individual or collective awareness of their leadership efficacy/identity. Ten students were interviewed and of those interviewed, eight had reached at least stage four of the model. The researcher established that all eight students had experienced some form of calamity, crisis, or significant challenge. For example, one student had transitioned to the United States from Turkey. She had overcome financial, familial, and cultural pressures to advance in her leadership abilities. She was able to articulate a clear interdependence on others in her organization. They needed each other as fellow leaders and relied on one another to accomplish the very challenging mission of their student organization (Durham Hynes, 2007).

The SCM and LID models hold that growth in leadership development is intimately connected with student learning and experience. "Leadership is not generally looked upon as a journey; yet leadership can be a developmental process that is clearly a transformational journey—a journey that has the potential to transform both the leader and ultimately those led" (Barbour & Hickman, 2011, p. 81). This is the common desire for both the student learning process and the development of leadership capacity in college students. "We are all, as colleagues and educators, now accountable to students and society for identifying and achieving essential student learning outcomes and for making transformative education possible and accessible for all students" (Keeling, 2004, p.1).

The SCM and LID models both assume that leadership is developed through "real life" experience. This is a critical assumption and supports the need to understand how experience shapes learning, specifically the learning of leadership. Perhaps one of the most important learning theories to understand as it relates to college student leadership development is Kolb's experiential learning theory, which posits that it is critical that students have a direct encounter with that which is being learned. Most readers of this text clearly understand that out-of-class experiences provide opportunities for students to have this type of direct encounter. For example, when a student learns from his/her advisor how to manage an organization meeting and then is able to practice this skill in the following week, experiential learning is taking place. Optimally, the student is then given feedback on his or her practice and can make improvements as needed. Students do not just study about something; they have a tangible experience with that which is being studied. Clearly experiential learning is natural in some disciplines like the hard sciences, where classroom learning is applied to laboratory experiments. Other disciplines have to be much more creative to incorporate experiential components. For example, the study of great philosophers does not make experiential learning automatic or easily accessible. However, a creative professor can bring to life something about the study to make the learning an experiential process for the students.

Kolb and Fry (1975) created their famous model of experiential learning from four elements, represented in the well-known experiential learning circle: (1) concrete experience, followed by (2) observation and reflection, followed by (3) forming abstract concepts, followed by (4) testing in new situations (Smith, 2001). From this model and the corresponding theory, four distinct learning styles were identified: converger, diverger, assimilator, and accommodator. See Table 1 for a description of each.

Table 1

Learning Styles

Learning Style	Learning Characteristic	Description
Converger	Abstract conceptualization + active experimentation	• Strong in practical application of ideas • Can focus on hypo-deductive reasoning on specific problems • Unemotional • Has narrow interests
Diverger	Concrete experience + reflective observation	• Strong in imaginative ability • Good at generating ideas and seeing things from different perspectives • Interested in people • Broad cultural interests
Assimilator	Abstract conceptualization + reflective observation	• Strong ability to create theoretical models • Excels in inductive reasoning • Concerned with abstract concepts rather than people
Accommodator	Concrete experience + active experimentation	• Greatest strength is doing things • More of a risk taker • Performs well when required to react to immediate circumstances • Solves problems intuitively

Although there are specific inventories that students can take to identify which learning style they resonate with most, professionals can also interpret something about a student's learning style or preference based on his or her academic discipline. Students who major in such disciplines as history, psychology, and fields in the arts and humanities generally have diverging learning styles, while those majoring in more abstract and applied areas like physics or engineering have converging learning styles (Kolb & Boyatzis, 2000). In both curricular and cocurricular experiences, extra effort should be applied to assess student learning styles and to incorporate a variety of experiences that allow each type of learner to succeed and master the content that is being presented. These types of varied learning experiences help students bridge theory and practice. It is not enough to present information in one format and assume that everyone in the room will be on an equal playing field in grasping the content that is being presented. For example, most institutions require student organizations to have a treasurer and for the treasurer to be knowledgeable about financial practices. While it may be assumed that all treasurers have basic awareness of these practices, a variety of procedures should be implemented at the institutional level and the specific organizational level to establish a baseline of financial knowledge amongst the treasurer cohort.

One example of an organization that has adopted a commitment to experiential learning is Outward Bound International. Speaking about their philosophy, Gerzon (2006) said, "Training does not take place in a classroom or with a case study. It takes place on a mountain cliff, on the ocean, or deep in a forest" (p. 205). Another example of experiential learning in action is the National 4-H model of learn by doing. According to this model, youth members of 4-H can have learning experiences that require minimal guidance from an adult. Students are encouraged to sort through a problem, identify a solution, and then act on it (Diem, 2001). Finally, from higher education comes the example of Grand Rapids Community College, which has established a Department of Experiential Learning. On its website (http://cms.grcc.edu/servicelearning), the department provides instructors with ideas and resources on implementing experiential learning within classroom and curricular experiences. Faculty and students can find resources on a range of experiences from one-time community service to recurrent service learning that is woven into a course or major. Such departments or centers at colleges and universities serve to centralize an important task: applying learning to life.

Case Update and Questions for Reflection

Mitch is two months into his presidency and things have seemed to go smoothly with the class officers to date. The first major class event is on the horizon, a class gathering that is held annually in conjunction with the junior class. The junior class advisor has just sent Mitch's advisor an e-mail saying that there are rumblings of trouble among the junior class officers. It appears that Mitch has taken a very aggressive role in planning the event, and other officers in both the sophomore and junior classes are put off by his approach. Given what his advisor knows about the SCM and LID models and how they integrate with Kolb's experiential learning theory, what should be the first steps in addressing this situation?

- How can the advisor encourage Mitch to share the load with other student leaders, perhaps giving them a chance to develop in their respective leadership abilities?
- How should the advisor respond to the junior class advisor who informed her of the situation?

Student Development Theory and Student Learning

In creating effective strategies for advancing individual student learning, it is useful to examine student development theory and how it interweaves with student learning, particularly experiential and transformative learning. With this framework, professionals can determine how best to assist students in the developmental process and create learning experiences that transcend the limitations of context and environment. While there are a number of theories that could be examined, perhaps the most relevant and timely are Chickering and Reisser's (1993) Seven Vectors that relate to college student identity development and Perry, Kohlberg, and Gilligan's developmental theories. These theories relate specifically to intellectual and moral development. Finally, it is helpful to look at the ways in which students make meaning of their experiences. Astin (1999) has done considerable work on documenting the value and importance of being engaged and involved in the learning experience, both inside and outside the classroom.

Chickering and Reisser's (1993) Seven Vectors flow out of Chickering's theory of identity development, which formed a framework for understanding common developmental steps that most college students experience. While not completely linear in nature, the vectors do appear to follow a stepwise path for most students. For the purposes of this chapter, each vector is briefly introduced and overlapping or intersecting points with student learning theories or concepts are explored. The first vector, developing competence, acknowledges that students will be developing in three domains during their college experience: intellectual; physical and manual skills; and interpersonal. It is important to note that the physical and manual skill development will most likely take place solely through more active and experiential forms of learning. In fields like nursing, there are inherent limitations to the learning process without delving into real-life experience. For example, although a nursing student can read and memorize information about blood vessels and blood pressure levels, actually learning the process of taking someone's blood pressure must involve hands-on experience. This is a manual skill and is foundational to many other pieces of practical nursing. Another example of physical or manual skill development is mastering basic word processing and other computer skills. In order to successfully perform in both in-class and out-of-class experiences, students must be able to use this technology. Because the current generation often has more skill in this area based on their secondary schooling, we may fall into the trap of assuming their skills. Advisors and instructors should assess students' knowledge and performance and provide instruction or opportunity for learning where needed.

While the vectors have been around for decades, perhaps the greatest affirmation of Chickering and Reisser's work has been shown recently as educators and scholars have developed a set of Essential Learning Outcomes for all college students (AAC&U, n.d.). One of these learning outcomes is themed "intellectual and practical skills, including . . . teamwork and problem solving" (AAC&U, n.d., p. 1). It can be assumed that students must have basic interpersonal competence in order to be able to work effectively with others in a team setting, regardless of the emphasis on problem solving.

The second vector in Chickering and Reisser's (1993) model is managing emotions. This vector assumes that students will experience a range of emotions during their lifetime and that their college experience will not be void of these emotions. Many students come to college with little awareness of their emotions, much less an ability to manage and channel them effectively. Educators can help students become more self-aware and honest with themselves about both positive and negative emotions that have been and will continue to be part of their experience. As mentioned earlier, transformative learning frames learning through four distinct frames of reference. Students can learn by elaborating on existing frames of reference or ways of knowing, by learning completely new frames of reference, by transforming existing points of view, and by transforming habits of the mind (Mezirow, 2000). The process of learning to manage emotions most likely combines at least two of these frames. Students who are becoming more aware of their emotions, both positive and negative, are developing a greater understanding of their existing frames of reference and may also be called on to transform habits of the mind. For example, if a student automatically becomes angry when someone disagrees with his/her point of view, even when disagreement is expressed in constructive ways, the student may have to form a brand new habit in order to expand his or her emotional repertoire.

The third vector of moving through autonomy toward interdependence involves learning self-sufficiency and agency. In this stage of development, students learn that they are in the driver's seat of their own development, and they cannot wait for someone else to provide experiences or situations in which they can learn. Also, students begin to understand that, although independence is important, interdependence is critical and a foundational principle for living effectively within our world. For example, students must come to understand that an employer who is evaluating their credentials after graduation is going to look for individual skills and achievements but will also want to know how the applicant can and will relate to others. In almost every field or industry, teamwork and healthy relationships are pivotal to performance success. In addition to these interdependence skills, the skills of agency, initiative, and problem solving are also developing in this critical stage of development. The SCM and LID models both point out the importance of groups and reliance on others, as well as the other skills mentioned above.

The fourth vector of developing mature interpersonal relationships overlaps somewhat with the previous vector in terms of working with others. This vector, however, takes the development of these relationships to a new level. Ideally, students will learn how to make meaningful commitments to others during this time of growth. Also, it is assumed that students will have the capacity to relate to those who are different from themselves, or at least have increased sensitivity in these relationships. In today's society, there is a more immediate need than ever before for this type of ability.

> In America . . . white males are supposedly the norm. Yet, in fact they are less than a third of the population and are becoming an ever-smaller percentage of the country. In such a world, getting along with people different from oneself is common sense. (Gerzon, 2006, p. 204)

Perhaps the most obvious area of intersection of vector four with the SCM is the value of controversy with civility. Students who have achieved an ability to have mature interpersonal relationships should also be able to navigate controversial situations with others holding civility as a constant. The developmental task of buildling mature interpersonal relationships is also consistent with the concept of Social Constructivism. Vygotsky, a Russian psychologist in the early 1900s, believed that all knowledge is socially constructed. It is built upon what people construct together and is reliant on what individuals contribute to the learning process (Hoy & Miskel, 2005).

In the fifth vector, establishing identity, Chickering and Reisser (1993) referenced Erikson's adolescent identity formation. Erikson described how adolescents begin to develop tolerance for others because they come to a place of peace and comfort with themselves (Chickering & Reisser). Baxter Magolda (2004) explained that excellence in life does not come automatically. College students must develop an integrated sense of themselves, cognitive maturity, and an ability to develop mature relationships across a variety of types of people. Chickering and Reisser, along with other theorists, posit that this vector is foundational work for young adults. Identity formation actually serves as the hinge for most if not all of the other vectors. If individuals do not have an accurate sense of themselves, they most likely will not have lasting, mature relationships.

In the two remaining vectors, Chickering and Reisser (1993) set out the tasks of developing purpose and developing integrity. Vector six, developing purpose, includes the process of defining aspirations and vocational goals. Here, students are integrating their understanding of self with their skills and abilities and developing plans for what they will do after college. They are also making more long-term plans for the kind of person that they want to be and the kinds of things that they want to achieve in their lifetime. One example of the ways in which students develop these long-term plans is listening to alumni who may come and present at their college or university. Many schools sponsor days or events where alumni come back to share how their educational experience made a difference in who they are today. For example, at Houghton College, a private Christian liberal arts institution, the career services office partners with the alumni relations office to sponsor vocational journey events. These events give students an opportunity to envision their own growth and development through the experiences of a professional who is in the work force, making a difference using their chosen vocation. While there are no clear places of overlap with the leadership models that we have discussed, the idea of "becoming a certain kind of person" is very consistent with the concept of self-authorship that will be explored in more detail in the next section of this chapter and again in Chapter 7.

The seventh and final vector is developing integrity. This task involves an exploration and a deepened understanding of how values and behaviors align. There is a high correlation between this vector and the value of congruence within the SCM. Also, in the fifth stage of the LID model, it is understood that people will be leading almost exclusively out of a place of generativity or leading with behaviors that involve reflection and making meaning of experiences. Also, in both the fifth and sixth stages of the LID model, leaders are very aware that their behaviors are being watched by others. They are trying to build leadership in others and, thus, there is a real awareness of the need for integrity and consistency between what the leader says and how the leader behaves.

As mentioned previously, it is important to briefly examine the works of Perry (1970), Kolhberg (1973), and Gilligan (1982) in light of their focus on intellectual and moral development. Perry's most notable contributions to our understanding of college student development came in his creation of nine stages of development. These nine stages identify how students move from being dualistic in their thinking (black and white, right and wrong), where knowledge is simply received and they do not yet know how to make meaning of knowledge, to being committed and able to integrate knowledge with personal experience and intentional reflection (Perry, 1970). Clearly, Perry's work informs much of our current understanding of leadership development, since almost any view or theory of postindustrial leadership acknowledges that leadership is a process and not an event. It is a process whereby the leader or a group of leaders must integrate what they know with what they believe and what they have experienced.

Kohlberg (1973) and Gilligan (1982) focused more exclusively on moral development in college students. It is important to briefly examine this work on moral development, given that SCM is based on values and LID is based on a grounded theory that incorporates how the leader understands himself or herself. Kohlberg's work focused on the study of men, establishing six distinct stages of moral development, while Gilligan advanced the work by including the study of college women. Table 2 shows Kohlberg's six stages of moral reasoning.

Table 2
Kohlberg's (1973) Moral Reasoning Stages

Stage 1	Obedience and punishment: Following rules helps me avoid punishment.
Stage 2	Individualism and exchange: I am most interested in serving my own needs.
Stage 3	Interpersonal relationships: I want to do what others expect of me; I want to please others.
Stage 4	Maintaining social order: I do what is expected of me in order to maintain order and obey the rules.
Stage 5	Social contract and individual rights: Rules are still important to me, but now I want people to be able to agree upon the rules, to have their opinions heard.
Stage 6	Universal principles: I am most concerned with ultimate justice. The rules are not as important to me anymore.

Gilligan (1982) took Piaget's (1950) foundational principles and studied a group of college women in order to develop her own stage theory of moral development. She maintained that there are three primary stages, preconventional, conventional, and postconventional, but she deviated from Kohlberg's (1973) work by proposing three total stages with two interspersed transitions. She also acknowledged that changes are fueled by an adjustment in the sense of self, not in cognitive capability as Kohlberg had suggested. Table 3 shows Gilligan's framework.

Table 3

Gilligan's (1982) Moral Development Stages

Stage 1	Goal: Individual survival
Transition from selfishness to responsibility to others	
Stage 2	Goal: Sacrificing one's self is good
Transition from goodness to truth	
Stage 3	Goal: Nonviolent principle (no harm to others or to self)

Perhaps the most important distinction between Kohlberg and Gilligan (aside from the fact that one studied men and one primarily studied women) is that each offers a unique approach to morality. Based on his work with men, Kohlberg (1973) posited that morality is built on a set of basic rights that can be acknowledged for all people. Gilligan (1982) stated that morality is based on responsibilities toward others and, therefore, the basis of the morality is an ethic of care for others. Most postindustrial views of leadership would probably be more congruent with Gilligan's approach to moral development, given that it seems to place a greater emphasis on relationships with others and on how these impact the development both of leaders and of those who follow.

Case Update and Questions for Reflection

It is now Mitch's fifth month of leadership of his class. The advisor has seen significant growth and development and is beginning to believe that Mitch is really turning a corner in his approach to leading others.

In a recent individual meeting with Mitch where the advisor and Mitch are discussing the spring semester, Mitch tells the advisor that one of his classes is giving him significant trouble at the start of this new semester. Although the class is not at all in the advisor's area of expertise, she listens intently as Mitch describes the challenging situation. Mitch explains that the class, an economics course that is part of the general education core at the college, is particularly difficult because there are a lot of "foreign" students in the class. Mitch says that he has been placed in a semester-long group assignment with four other students, three of whom do not come from the United States and two of whom have thick accents, most likely because English is not their first language. Mitch says that the group asked him to be the group leader, and he is very grateful for this role. That being said, he is struggling to bring the group together given their differences. In their first group meeting, they got into a tense discussion about politics, and Mitch believes that a couple of the group members walked away angry from the discussion. The second group meeting is on the horizon, and Mitch is stressed out about it. He fears that he is going to be stuck doing all of the work for the group because he is the leader. He asks for the advisor's advice on how to get through this difficult situation. What developmental work might be happening for Mitch right now? (Consider all of the areas of development that have been touched on in this chapter: identity, intellectual, moral, leadership, learning, etc.).

- How can the advisor help make connections between the growth and improvement she has seen in his leadership skills as class president and the situation that he is presenting to her from his coursework?
- What initial steps might Mitch take to be effective as the positional leader of this group? How can the advisor encourage him to share leadership with others and not take on the responsibility of doing all of the work?

Self-Authorship

People compose their own stories about who they are, what life is about, what is going to happen to them, and how they should respond to the various challenges they encounter. Maturation or development occurs as people become more capable of articulating and critiquing personal stories, reframing these stories, and reshaping their own lives. As college students are developing, one of the culminating tasks they should work through is self-authorship, or the task of internally coordinating beliefs, values, and interpersonal loyalties rather than depending on external values, beliefs, and interpersonal loyalties (Baxter Magolda & King, 2004). Self-authorship requires students to have epistemological maturity and requires cultivating a secure sense of self that allows for interdependent relationships with others and for making judgments through considering, but not being consumed by, others' perspectives (Kegan, 1994). This concept grows out of the work by Kegan (1994) and Baxter Magolda and King

(2004), all of whom have written widely on the concept and its application to work with students. Kegan (1994) and Baxter Magolda (1999) considered self-authorship a process of reframing and reshaping experiences into an integrated story that helps to shape how the individual will respond to future situations. They indicated that self-authorship is one of the higher levels of the developmental process, a way of making meaning in which people reflect on their lives, their values, and their behavior and consider whether or not previous choices remain useful or productive for them. "Frames of reference—and, therefore, students' stories—change with growth, emerging or fading in a non-linear way" (Keeling, 2004, p. 9).

Three questions that individuals ask in the journey toward self-authorship are (1) How do I know? (2) Who am I? and (3) How do I want to construct relationships with others? The college experience in totality is helpful to students in answering these questions, which correspond to the three dimensions of self-authorship: epistemological, intrapersonal, and interpersonal. Dimensions intertwine and interrelate depending on the unique experiences of every individual. Baxter Magolda defined the intersection point of the three dimensions as the *inner voice* (Baxter Magolda & King, 2004). Scharmer (2008) wrote:

> We know a great deal about *what* leaders do and how they do it. But we know very little about the inner place, the source from which they operate. Successful leadership depends on the quality of attention and intention that the leaders bring to any situation. (p. 52)

While students are ultimately responsible for their choices and the amount of effort that they bring to the learning experience, educators are responsible for creating an environment that is conducive to the highest and deepest level of learning possible. In a paper presented at Mosakowski Institute for Public Enterprise, Hodge, Baxter Magolda, and Haynes (2009) provided a new model for colleges and universities to consider, the engaged learning environment. This model takes learning beyond being simply integrated to also being sequenced and increasing steadily in levels of challenge for students. The engaged learning environment "assumes students can develop into mature scholars and citizens if educators provide a coherent, sequenced curriculum and co-curriculum" (Hodge, Baxter Magolda, & Haynes, 2009, p. 9). This model brings together the best of leadership and learning theories as it transcends concepts from transformative and experiential learning, intellectual and moral developmental models, identity development tasks, and postindustrial models of leadership. "The engaged learning environment fosters the epistemological, intrapersonal, and interpersonal developmental capacities that enable learners to participate in discovery and interdependent knowledge construction" (Hodge, Baxter Magolda, & Hanes, 2009, pp. 9–10).

This model is an extension of what Baxter Magolda and King (2004) had previously offered in the Learning Partnerships Model, in which colleges and universities were called on to create environments between individuals and authorities that promote self-authorship. The Learning Partnerships Model described an ideal college or university environment in which students are enabled to interact with both their peers and educators; have space for self-reflection and time for determining beliefs and values; and experience active learning and involvement within meaningful activities. It almost sounds utopian, but this type of learning environment is possible when planned for through intentional means and methods. Such a learning environment is possible at any type of institution, but it requires all educators to go through a transformational process as well. Consider a community college environment where students are challenged to apply learning from the classroom and from life experiences to service experiences that are offered in the cocurriculum. Consider a liberal arts institution where the capstone course taken in the senior year not only integrates content from the students' primary discipline, but also incorporates leadership and service experiences that have been completed through the cocurriculum.

It is important to remember that the concept of the engaged learning environment will only be possible if students are set on a path to self-authorship. Ultimately, a student body that is equipped with developmental gains in this area will be more receptive and capable of becoming mature scholars and citizens.

Practicing Learning

We can easily acknowledge that students are constantly learning. Some say that students in the college environment are bound to learn, no matter how carelessly the experiences are planned for or executed. That being said, this random and by-chance learning is insufficient and may leave a student ill-prepared for the world in which they are going to live and work. Educators must become purposeful about everything in the college experience and capitalize on each facet of the student's educational encounter. In the best-case scenario, this purposeful planning is coordinated across the institution, and students experience a seamless learning environment where there is consistency and synergy within and between experiences. A student's work-study job on campus should not be simply a means of financial support while going to school. It should ultimately contain clear learning outcomes that contribute to and integrate with the overall learning objectives of the college experience as a whole. While this might seem out of reach, there are institutions that are thinking in integrated ways about the learning experience. For example, Miami University has developed a set of tiered learning outcomes for students in their honors program. These outcomes transcend the classroom and allow students to integrate each dimension of their campus experience into the overall learning process.

Conclusion

Ultimately, colleges and universities are trying to prepare students to influence the world, to have the ability to continue to learn and develop, and to make lasting contributions to their respective fields or disciplines. I would call these students leaders. While not everyone may automatically deem these graduates to be leaders, I believe that those who undertake this set of tasks are living out several, if not all, of the values presented in the Social Change Model of Leadership Development and will most likely have advanced into the interdependent stages of the Leadership Identity Development Model. In preparing these leaders, we must remember that "the best leaders work from a place of integrity in themselves, from their hearts" (Palmer, 2001, p. 27). We have the privileged role of helping students learn how to be leaders who practice the work of leading from their hearts, from their true selves.

Case Conclusion and Final Questions for Reflection

It is the end of the year, and Mitch has seen his position through to completion. The next set of officers has been selected, and Mitch is preparing to pass on the mantle of leadership. He chose not to run again for a position because he wants to focus his time and energy on preparing for work after college through an internship. He asks his advisor to help him prepare the next set of class officers. In the closing meeting, the advisor also works through a review of the goals that Mitch had eventually set at the beginning of the year. Both the advisor and Mitch are pleased with how the year has ultimately gone.

Questions for Reflection

1. What steps would you take in helping Mitch reflect on his year?
2. What goals is Mitch setting for his future? How can you help him translate his learning from this leadership experience into his internship and other future opportunities?
3. How have you grown or developed as an advisor because of your experiences with Mitch this year?
4. What would you do differently if you were given the chance to do the year over again?
5. How can we reconcile the importance of success in leading others with the value of failure and what it can teach not only the leader but the followers as well? For example, when do we allow student leaders to fail, even if it could have negative repercussions on a group of students or even on the institution as a whole? Parker Palmer, in his book *The Active Life* (1991), said,

   > Our successes and our glories are not the stuff of community, but our sins and our failures are. In those difficult areas of our lives we confront the human condition, and we begin to learn compassion for all beings who share the limits of life itself. (p. 31)

6. How should leadership and learning differ, if at all, based on the type of institution in which the development is taking place? Does it matter if a student is of a traditional or nontraditional age? How do we support the development of leadership and learning in a culture where it may not be valued as highly due to other priorities or an unclear mission connection?
7. What barriers stand in the way of creating an engaged learning environment on your campus? What can you do personally, within your sphere of influence, to move your institution closer to this goal?

References

Alliance for Excellent Education. (2008). *International comparisons of academic achievement.* Retrieved from http://www.all4ed.org/files/IntlComp_FactSheet.pdf

Allio, R. J. (2005). Leadership development: teaching versus learning. *Management Decision, 43*(7), 1071–1077.

Association of American Colleges and Universities (AACU&U). (n.d.). *The essential learning outcomes.* Retrieved from http://www.aacu.org/leap/documents/EssentialOutcomes_Chart.pdf

Astin, A. W. (1999). Student involvement: A developmental theory for higher education. *Journal of College Student Development, 40*(5), 518–529.

Barbour, J. D., & Hickman, G. R. (2011). (Eds.). *Leadership for transformation.* San Francisco, CA: Jossey-Bass.

Baxter Magolda, M. B., & King, P. (2004). *Making their own way.* Sterling, VA: Stylus Publishing.

Chickering, A. W., & Reisser, L. (1993). *Education and Identity.* San Francisco, CA: Jossey- Bass.

Denzin, N. K., & Lincoln, Y. S. (2003). (Eds.). *Turning points in qualitative research: Turning knots in a handkerchief.* Blue Ridge Summit, PA: Alta Mira Press.

DeZure, D. (2000). *Learning from Change: Landmarks in teaching and learning in higher education from Change magazine, 1969–1999.* Sterling, VA: Stylus Publishing.

Diem, K. (2001). The learn-by-doing approach to life skill development. Retrieved from the Rutgers NJAES Cooperative Extension website: http://njaes.rutgers.edu/pubs/publication.asp?pid=fs891

Durham Hynes, S. L. (2007). *Perceptions of the capacity for change as a component of leadership development as reported by select populations of college students: Implications for college student leadership development* (Doctoral dissertation). Available from ProQuest Dissertations and Theses database. (UMI No. 3370691)

Gerzon, M. (2006). *Leading through conflict: How successful leaders transform differences into opportunities.* Boston, MA: Harvard Business Review Press.

Gilligan, C. (1982). *In a different voice: Psychological theory and women's development.* Cambridge, MA: Harvard University Press.

Higher Education Research Institute (HERI). (1996). *A social change model of leadership development* (Version III). Los Angeles, CA: Author.

Hodge, D. C., Baxter Magolda, M. B., & Haynes, C. A. (2009). Engaged learning: Enabling self-authorship and effective practice. *Liberal Education, 95*(4), 16–23.

Hoy, W. K. & Miskel, C. G. (2005). *Educational Administration.* New York, NY: McGraw Hill Publishers.

Keeling, R. P. (Ed.). (2004). *Learning reconsidered: A campus-wide focus on the student experience.* Washington, DC: American College Personnel Association and National Association of Student Personnel Administrators.

Kegan, R. (1994). *In over our heads: The mental demands of modern life.* Cambridge, MA: Harvard University Press.

Kientz, J. A., Arriaga, R. I., Chetty, M., Hayes, G. R., Richardson, J., Patel, S. N., & Abowd, G. D. (2007). Grow and know: Understanding record-keeping needs for tracking the development of young children. Proceedings of the SIGCHI Conference on Human Factors in Computing Systems, San Jose, CA, 1351–1360. doi: 10.1145/1240624.1240830

Kohlberg, L. (1973). The claim to moral adequacy of a highest stage of moral judgment. *Journal of Philosophy, 70*(18), 630–646.

Kolb, D. A., & Boyatzis, R. E. (2000). Experiential learning theory: Previous research and new directions. In R. J. Sternberg & L. F. Zhang (Eds.), *Perspectives on thinking, learning, and cognitive styles.* Mahwah, NJ: Lawrence Erlbaum.

Kolb, D. A., & Fry, R. (1975). Toward an applied theory of experiential learning. In C. Cooper (Ed.), *Theories of Group Process.* London, England: John Wiley.

Komives, S. R., Casper, J. O., Longerbeam, S., Mainella, F. C., & Osteen, L. (2004, March). Developing a leadership identity: A grounded theory. Handout from presentation at National Association of Student Personnel Administrators Annual Conference: Denver, CO.

Komives, S. R., & Wagner, W. (2009). *Leadership for a better world.* San Francisco, CA: Jossey-Bass.

Mashek, D., & Hammer, E. (2011). *Empirical research in teaching and learning contributions from social psychology.* Malden, MA: Blackwell Publishing.

Mezirow, J. (Ed.). (2000). *Learning as transformation: Critical perspectives on a theory in progress.* San Francisco, CA: Jossey-Bass.

Mitchell, R. L. (2006). Emanation and generation. *About Campus, 11*(5), 29–30.

Northouse, P. G. (2004). *Leadership theory and practice.* Thousand Oaks, CA: Sage Publications.

Palmer, P. (1991). *The active life.* San Francisco, CA: Jossey-Bass.

Palmer, P. (2001, Fall). Leadership and the inner journey. *Leader to Leader,* 26–33.

Perry, W. G., Jr. (1970). *Forms of intellectual and ethical development in the college years: A scheme.* New York, NY: Holt, Rinehart, and Winston.

Piaget, J. (1950). The psychology of intelligence (M. Piercy & D. E. Berlyne, Trans.). London, England: Routledge & Kegan Paul.

Scharmer, C. O. (2008, Winter). Uncovering the blind spot of leadership. *Leader to Leader,* 52–59.

Smith, M. K. (2001). David A. Kolb on experiential learning. *The Encyclopedia of Informal Education (infed).* Retrieved from http://www.infed.org/biblio/b-explrn.htm#learning%20style

Social Change Model. (2011). Social change model. Retrieved from http://www.thesocialchangemodel.org

Sykes, C. J. (1995). *Dumbing down our kids: Why America's children feel good about themselves but can't read, write, or add.* New York, NY: St. Martin's Griffin.

Tennant, M. (1997). *Psychology and adult learning.* London, England: Routledge.

Zimmerman-Oster, K., & Burkhardt, J. C. (1999). *Leadership in the making: Impact and insights from leadership development programs in U.S. colleges and universities.* Battle Creek, MI: Kellogg Foundation Monograph.

CHAPTER 3

DETERMINING SKILLS AND OUTCOMES

What Should Student Leaders Know or Be Able to Do?

Peggy C. Holzweiss

As highlighted in Chapter 1, higher education constituents are increasing their demands for accountability regarding what students learn in college and how that learning equates to sufficient knowledge and skill development leading to paying jobs. These demands grow greater every year due to the rising costs of a college education. Yet, as pointed out in Chapter 2, learning is unique for each college student, and it is difficult to create a one-size-fits-all approach for the assessment of learning. Even in an academic discipline, each course has its own set of outcomes, and those outcomes may shift as research and practice defines the field. Applied on a larger scale, capturing student learning is a challenging endeavor.

What is learned, how it is learned, and how students process the information are all influenced by a variety of factors such as federal and state government policies, religious affiliation, accrediting agency demands, and industry needs for a skilled workforce. As these influences swirl around each college and university, the focus must remain on the institutional mission and on what students on that campus are to learn from their education. Institutions are individually accountable to the students they serve while also balancing the requirements and needs of their other constituents such as alumni and the business community. The daunting task of determining skills and outcomes can only be addressed by bringing the focus to a local level and examining how all of the outside influences can be melded successfully with desired student learning outcomes identified by the institution and the opportunities it offers.

While creating learning outcomes can be challenging to all who attempt to write them, academic units have an inherent advantage because the classroom environment requires a clear statement of what is to be gained from participating in a course. Classroom activities, textbooks, and assignments cannot be planned without plainly understanding the desired end result. In addition, the majority of students who enroll in the course share a common need to fulfill a step along their academic path, whether through completing a requirement or obtaining an elective. Student affairs, on the other hand, must define learning in an environment where tests are not administered, papers are not assigned, and no accrediting body defines what students who participate in the activities should learn. Also, the students who join activities sponsored by student affairs vary. They range from students serving in leadership positions within student organizations to resident advisors who are paid to supervise at residence halls. These students have a variety of motivations and needs, such as finding a sense of belonging, pursuing hobbies, obtaining a regular paycheck, and learning new skills.

Arnold and Kuh (1999) noted that faculty and student affairs differ on the very definition of learning: Faculty prepare students for a product (knowledge) while student affairs focuses on guiding them through a process that never ends. Even though the approach to learning may be different, learning is the responsibility of all who work in higher education, both inside and outside the classroom (Whitt, 2006). As Keeling, Wall, Underhile, and Dungy (2008) explained:

> There is no assumption that students gain all of their new capacities, competencies, or skills in any area—such as critical thinking—from one course, or just in the major; nor do students learn everything they will come to know about leadership from the leadership development activities offered in student affairs. Overall institutional learning outcomes are exactly that—the products of students' entire engagement with every aspect of the institution (that is, with all of the resources that the institution has gathered, allocated, and integrated to support the education and preparation of the whole student). (pp. 7–8)

With no clear road map and different forms of learning taking place throughout the campus community, how should student affairs professionals determine what student leaders should know or be able to do at the conclusion of a wide variety of cocurricular activities such as living on campus, participating in student organizations, or conducting community service? What cocurricular learning outcomes will meet the demands of institutional accountability and higher education constituents while also matching the expectations of faculty for what students should learn? In order to understand what learning outcomes are relevant in a diverse environment, it is first important to review the evolution of the cocurricular life of students.

History and Importance of the Cocurricular Environment

When higher education began in the United States, its purpose was to turn young men into clergy or public leaders (Cohen, 1998). This purpose was accomplished by focusing on classical subjects and religious teachings and by carefully monitoring student life outside of the classroom (Sheldon, 1901). As the new nation expanded westward, societal interest in topics such as industry and science grew (Cohen, 1998), yet the college curriculum did not adapt to changing interests (Sheldon, 1901). Students responded by forming literary societies where they could direct their own learning through participating in debates and collecting and reading new literature that was not covered in the classroom. Rudolph (1990) noted:

> In a sense, the literary societies and their libraries, the clubs, journals, and organizations which compensated for the neglect of science, English literature, history, music, and art in the curriculum—this vast developing extracurriculum was the student response to the classical course of study. It brought prestige to the life of the mind. It helped to liberate the intellect on the American campus. It was one answer to the Yale Report of 1828, an answer so effective that by the end of the century at Yale itself, there would be real concern over which was really more fundamental, which more important, the curriculum or the extracurriculum. (p. 144)

One historical account of literary societies even identified the skills that were developed by members of these organizations, including communication, meeting management, and critical thinking (Sheldon, 1901).

While the faculty initially attempted to suppress the activities of the literary societies, other changes in the higher education environment moved them toward joining the students in pursuit of intellectual development. The most influential event in shifting the focus of the faculty was the founding of Johns Hopkins University in 1876, which was created to reflect the German model of higher education, with a clear focus on research and the development of new knowledge (Cohen, 1998). With this new model of higher education, faculty were prized not for their adherence to traditional curriculum and religion, but for conducting research that solved societal problems (Cohen, 1998).

Because faculty were now focusing on the pursuit of intellectual development, the literary societies decreased in importance while other student organizations emerged to fulfill growing developmental needs (Rudolph, 1990). These new groups included social fraternities and Greek societies to help students network more effectively and build friendships and secret societies to give students greater influence on the campus political process (Sheldon, 1901). In addition, literary societies morphed into different types of organizations such as debating societies and professional associations focusing on the career fields of medicine, law, and science (Sheldon, 1901). The German gymnasium movement spurred a growth in recreational groups, and student government associations formed to provide students an opportunity to share student perspectives on campus issues (Rudolph, 1990). Students also were still living on campus in large numbers, so residence halls formed the basis of many smaller communities that provided support for academic and personal needs.

Clearly, the history of cocurricular involvement provides numerous examples of students creating opportunities to learn and grow when the formal academic environment fell short of their expectations. One conclusion Pascarella and Terenzini (2005) drew after 30 years of research was that "failure to capitalize on students' out-of-class experiences risks increasing learning only at the margins" (p. 647). The researchers recommended that institutions strive to have a seamless learning environment and find ways to bridge formal and informal educational opportunities in order to create a higher level of engagement by each student. These bridge opportunities could include partnerships between faculty and student affairs professionals in areas such as student organization involvement, study abroad activities, or campus governance. This recommendation was reiterated by Keeling, et al. (2008), who suggested that student affairs professionals create a formal strategy for student learning in order to capture the development that occurs outside of the classroom.

Defining What Is Important

So how can student affairs turn the cocurricular environment into intentional learning? The first place to look for guidance is the set of organizational statements; institutional mission, vision, goals, and values. These statements provide valuable guidance as to what is important for the campus, and constructs a solid foundation on which to build. Once students affairs has a thorough understanding of the institution, Huba and Freed

(2000) recommended taking a systems approach that involves a variety of partners. For instance, one cocurricular experience is being engaged in student organizations. Student organizations have members, leaders, and staff advisors, and all of them need specific skills in order to perform well in their roles. In addition, advisors have supervisors who support their professional performance and development, so they, too, should be included in the systematic approach to student learning. Many student affairs staff also supervise student employees, another set of students who engage in learning.

Once partners have been identified, each role should be examined to ascertain the skill sets and competencies inherent in those roles. For example, members of a group may need to learn how to follow directions, accept and perform delegated tasks, participate effectively in meetings and other activities, and contribute to the mission and goals of the organization. Leaders may need to learn how to communicate with one other, the advisor, their members, and a variety of outside constituents. They may also need to learn meeting management, event management, supervision, delegation skills, and how to provide critical feedback.

Along with the general skills needed for members and leaders, an examination of organizational processes may reveal additional areas for learning. For instance, organizations may engage in a selection process for members and leaders. What skills do potential members need to have in order to perform well in the organization? For each leadership position, what skills may be required to meet the identified responsibilities? How are these skills explored through the application and interview processes? How are final selections made, and what skills are involved in this process? What kind of training do new members and leaders receive, and who organizes and implements this training? Delving into the activities of an organization can help identify additional skills and competencies that may be part of the learning process.

The same process can be applied to advisors and their supervisors. Advisors, whether full time, part time, assigned, or voluntary, may need to enhance their supervision and facilitation skills so they can better guide student leaders to embrace their own learning and skill development. The organizations they advise, however, can be quite different and may require additional competencies for effective management. For instance, student organizations that are focused on cultural issues may need an advisor who is well versed in the diversity literature and can identify special concerns the students may encounter. The advisor could also have a second assignment with a residence hall governance organization, which requires knowledge of parliamentary procedure. The training needs of the advisor should be tailored to the needs of the organizations as well as the current knowledge and background of the advisor. It should not be assumed that years of experience with advising student groups equates to knowing everything required by each organization.

Although the advisor is the person who must acquire these specific sets of knowledge and learn to use them effectively with students, the advisor's supervisor must also participate in the process. Supervisors may need to suggest appropriate professional development opportunities to their staff members, create a professional performance plan that captures student learning goals and responsibilities, and reward the advisors when the performance plan is executed. Supervisors of all backgrounds may require additional training in order to fully understand student learning and its impact, set expectations for staff members who help create the environment for student learning, guide staff members through the intentional implementation of student learning tasks, and hold advisors accountable.

Identifying all possible local partners and their needs is a good starting point, but to truly create a seamless learning environment, it is necessary to align what can and should be gained in cocurricular activities with other campus and professional sources. These sources could include the institutional mission, vision, and goals; accreditation agencies; professional associations; federal and state government initiatives, publications, and organizations; industry needs; faculty; student affairs professionals; former students; and current students. All of these sources will be explored further in this chapter.

Institutional Mission, Vision, and Goals

According to Evers, Rush, and Berdrow (1998), "Every college and university has a unique character and niche. We believe that the best process for implementing a move to increasing skill development begins with analyzing the organizations' vision, mission, and niche" (p. 154). Kuh, Kinzie, Schuh, and Whitt (2005) further explained that every institution has two missions: the publicly shared mission and the one that is addressed by the actions the institution takes on a daily basis. These two missions may not be completely aligned if stated expectations are not supported by regular practice.

If student affairs is to help create a seamless learning environment, its practices must be aligned with what the institutional mission, vision, and goals espouse. One study of chief academic officers nationwide reveals that three-quarters of all institutions have a common set of learning outcomes for undergraduate students, created to meet the stated goals of their campuses and to meet demands from accreditors (Kuh & Ikenberry, 2009). Accrediting agencies use what colleges say about themselves in order to understand whether or not the colleges are meeting the goals they set for themselves. Institutions have the freedom to create student learning outcomes that match the purpose of the offered education as long as all pieces align clearly.

One example of how learning outcomes can be created from the public statements describing an institution comes from Miami Dade College. According to its website, "The mission of Miami Dade College is to change lives through the opportunity of education" by providing "high-quality teaching and learning experiences that are accessible and affordable to meet the needs of our diverse students and prepare them to be responsible global citizens and successful lifelong learners" (Miami Dade College, n.d.a, para. 1–2). This mission statement is similar to those held by other institutions. In fact, if the name of the college were not provided, it would be hard to determine what institution it described. The mission statement by itself does not provide enough substance to form a true foundation for student learning, but it does offer a starting point to understand the direction the institution wishes to go.

More details governing how the institution sees itself are necessary before one can determine what students should know or be able to do when they complete their education. Examining the vision statement for Miami Dade College provides several indicators for the competencies and skills students should gain at the institution. The actual statement, which also doubles as the institution's stated values, covers a variety of areas, including ideas such as "an exceptional learning environment" highlighting innovation and offering students both challenge and support; "a culture of inquiry and evidence" accomplished through student learning outcomes and assessment measures; "quality community partnerships" that provide community service opportunities; "a commitment to cultural initiatives" that accentuate the arts and multiculturalism; and "global reach and awareness," which provide international context and understanding (Miami Dade College, n.d.a, para. 3).

In 2007, Miami Dade College took these statements and created a Learning Outcomes Covenant in which students agree to be mindful of their learning and to participate in the pursuit of learning outcomes and the faculty agree to address the learning outcomes in their courses and work to engage the students in learning (Miami Dade College, n.d.b). The covenant is followed by a list of student learning outcomes that align with the mission and vision statements:

- Communicate effectively using listening, speaking, reading, and writing skills.
- Use quantitative analytical skills to evaluate and process numerical data.
- Solve problems using critical and creative thinking and scientific reasoning.
- Formulate strategies to locate, evaluate, and apply information.
- Demonstrate knowledge of diverse cultures, including global and historical perspectives.
- Create strategies that can be used to fulfill personal, civic, and social responsibilities.

- Demonstrate knowledge of ethical thinking and its application to issues in society.
- Use computer and emerging technologies effectively.
- Demonstrate an appreciation for aesthetics and creative activities.
- Describe how natural systems function and recognize the impact of humans on the environment. (Miami Dade College, n.d.b, para. 7)

The learning outcomes Miami Dade College created match the stated mission and vision of the institution and provide a road map for any academic or service unit on what students should know or be able to do. In fact, a quick scan of many of the institution's web pages reveals that every unit, service, and resource adheres to or promotes the learning outcomes—including student affairs areas such as arts, culture, and study abroad activities. Student learning permeates the institution, and every corner of the college is expected to participate in the development of students.

Accrediting Agencies and Professional Associations

Miami Dade College stands out because of its learner-centered environment, but many institutions do not take the time to fully develop student learning outcomes and create such a culture. In fact, as noted previously, institutions often create student learning outcomes because it is expected by accreditation agencies (Kuh & Ikenberry, 2009). When institutions join these agencies, they agree to meet the standards set forth by these independent, nongovernmental entities (Upcraft & Schuh, 1996). The agencies conduct periodic reviews of each member institution, and if they meet all of the standards, the institutions are granted formal accreditation. This status is desirable because it contributes to a strong institutional or program reputation and communicates to the public that independent and specific standards for the academic environment have been met. Of course, accrediting agencies must focus on specific requirements due to resource constraints, so institutions may not put as much time into areas outside of those requirements. However, understanding what the accrediting agencies are looking for can help student affairs identify where it might assist the academic units with obtaining the accreditation.

There are a variety of agencies that offer accreditation to higher education institutions. For instance, some faith-based institutions may choose to become members of the Association of Independent Christian Colleges and Seminaries while colleges with a liberal arts focus may wish to join the American Academy for Liberal Education. Public colleges and universities may belong to one of several regional accrediting agencies across the United States, such as the Middle States Association of Colleges and Schools Commission on Higher Education, the Northwest Commission on Colleges and Universities, and the Western Association of Schools and Colleges Accrediting Commission for Senior Colleges and Universities.

Middaugh (2010) examined the requirements of these public regional agencies and found similarities among them. For instance, student learning requirements for the agencies included demonstrating the knowledge, skills, and competencies that students develop while at the institution, as well as demonstrating how the acquired abilities align with institutional goals. Accrediting agencies also expect assessment of institutional effectiveness and a systematic strategic planning process. Institutions that cannot validate their student learning claims risk possible withdrawal of accreditation, which can harm the institutional reputation and send potential students to other campuses. These standards can help institutions further define and measure student learning in the variety of environments found on a college campus.

Accrediting agencies exist for a variety of institutional types (e.g., community colleges, faith-based institutions, and private and public institutions) or academic disciplines (e.g., nursing, engineering, business, etc.). For example, ABET, formerly known as the Accreditation Board for Engineering and Technology, provides quality assurance for academic programs in applied science, computer science, engineering, and technology (ABET, 2010). Standards are set by the different professionals who work in these fields. As its website indicates, ABET accreditation is needed to help students identify quality academic programs and prepare them for careers and to provide standards for continuous evaluation of the learning environment (ABET, 2010). While ABET closely monitors the curriculum content for these academic programs, it does not stop at knowledge standards. The criteria for accreditation in engineering include general skills such as analyzing and interpreting data, identifying and solving problems, acting in a professional and ethical manner, working successfully in groups, communicating effectively, and practicing lifelong learning. By reviewing and acknowledging the transferable skills outlined by accreditation agencies, student affairs can assist students in bridging what is required of a specific career field and what is learned through cocurricular activities.

Similar to accreditation agencies, many professional associations publish desired competencies by discipline such as nursing, psychology, athletic coaching, and human resources. In 1996, the American College Personnel Association (ACPA) published the *Student Learning Imperative,* which was designed to promote critical thinking on how student learning could be enhanced throughout student affairs. While the ACPA document sparked conversations about student learning, the Council for the Advancement of Standards in Higher Education (CAS) went one step further and identified standards for numerous specialties within student affairs, such as alcohol and drug education programs, career services, honor societies, college unions, international student programs, and student conduct programs (CAS, 2010). For example, the CAS standards for fraternity and sorority advising include competencies such as critical thinking, self-understanding, interpersonal skills, civic engagement, technical competence, and maintaining health and wellness (Association of Fraternity/Sorority Advisors, 2009).

While CAS standards were developed over time to guide specific areas of student affairs (CAS, 2010), standards can also be identified by publications that are responding to the changing educational environment. One such publication, *Learning Reconsidered* (Keeling, 2004), addressed the increasing need for student affairs to collaborate with academic affairs in order to promote a seamless learning environment. Among the competencies the document highlighted were integrating classroom learning with cocurricular experiences, forming personal identity and self-understanding, increasing cultural competency, collaborating with others, demonstrating self-sufficiency, and improving communication. Another publication from the Association of American Colleges and Universities (AAC&U) (2007) supported these identified competencies and noted that "educational communities will also have to become far more intentional themselves—both about the kinds of learning students need, and about effective educational practices that help students learn to integrate and apply their learning" (p. 5).

Building on the CAS standards, ACPA and the National Association of Student Personnel Administrators (NASPA) jointly published *Professional Competency Areas for Student Affairs Practitioners* (2010), a guide intended to promote the knowledge and skills needed for a career in the field. The identified competency areas cover topics such as advising, assessment, diversity, ethics, law, leadership, and student development. In addition to identifying areas of potential growth for professionals, the resource highlights specific outcomes at the basic, intermediate, and advanced levels so individuals, supervisors, and units can ascertain where additional training and development might be needed.

Federal Government

The changing educational environment that prompted these publications is often driven by political leaders who see a need for reform. For example, in 1990, the state governors responded to corporations and policymakers who were concerned about the abilities of college graduates who joined the workforce (Jones, 1995). These groups believed that graduates were not meeting expectations in the areas of critical thinking and communication and that a solution had to be found on a national level to ensure graduates met basic competencies.

In an effort to address these concerns, researchers at the National Center for Education Statistics asked national experts in assessment and student learning to identify specific skills that could better define these competencies. The process revealed that even experts could not agree on what skills properly defined critical thinking and communication and that the best approach would be to provide a list of skills "that can be reviewed and considered by faculty, employers, and policymakers" (Jones, 1995, p. 4). One interesting conclusion of this process was that "students must become more engaged in their own learning in order to help them develop their advanced skills" (Jones, 1995, p. 165). The researchers also highlighted their finding that, in order to truly understand whether or not students were developing skills, learning had to be measured through the application of skills outside the classroom environment.

Following this exercise, the U.S. Secretary of Labor formed the Secretary's Commission on Achieving Necessary Skills to interview employers, union officials, and employees of a variety of businesses in order to ascertain what high school students should know or be able to do upon graduation. The skills and competencies highlighted by this study included allocating resources, teaching others, serving customers, organizing and maintaining files, speaking, listening, reading, writing, and monitoring and correcting performance (U.S. Department of Labor, 1991). The recommendations of the commission included sharing expectations for learning with students, evaluating them and sharing the results of the evaluation, and incorporating skill-based learning in every aspect of the educational institution.

In 2006, the U.S. Department of Education, under the direction of Secretary Margaret Spellings, extended a similar educational evaluation to institutes of higher education. The resulting Report of the Secretary of Education's Commission on the Future of Higher Education (commonly referred to as the "Spellings Report") outlined the decreasing quality of American higher education and called for greater innovation and improved accountability (U.S. Department of Education, 2006). While the report noted that colleges and universities had been increasing the focus on student learning, it leveled criticisms that no real evidence had been provided regarding what students learned. The subsequent administration, led by President Barack Obama, similarly emphasized that higher education should be doing more to help students succeed, including teaching high-demand skills so that industries can gain the workforce they need to succeed (White House, n.d.).

State Government

It is important for student affairs professionals to pay attention to actions and statements from the federal government because they often precede what happens on the state level. While national political leaders continue to call for improvements to the K–16 system, it is the state governments that must create and lead reforms on the local level. One important example of how a state government can influence student learning within its higher education institutions comes from South Dakota. Structurally, South Dakota has a Board of Regents for the University System whose members are appointed by the governor and confirmed by the state Senate (Martinez, 1999). This board provides oversight and strategic planning for public colleges in the state, as well as setting tuition rates. In 1995, the board initiated roundtable discussions with business leaders, K–12 educators, policymakers, and higher education representatives. This discussion opened up dialogue regarding the challenges for improving higher education and creating tangible benefits for the state, businesses, and citizens (Martinez, 1999).

In an effort to improve the effectiveness of higher education, these roundtable discussions led to the creation of the Regental Proficiency Examination that is aligned with the national ACT exam that South Dakota requires for admission to its public institutions (Martinez, 1999). The exam, given to sophomores, is required in order for students to progress to their upper-level academic courses (South Dakota Board of Regents, n.d.). The exam covers such skills as writing, math, science reasoning, and reading, all of which are included in a requirement in the core academic curriculum for students enrolled in public institutions. If a student does not pass the minimum standards for the exam on the initial or second try, he or she must meet with an assigned advisor to create a development plan to improve the competencies in question. Any student not achieving a passing score on the exam after retest is denied subsequent registration at all public institutions in the state.

This midpoint exam benefits a variety of constituents. For instance, it allows each institution to track the progress of individual students and intervene at a point where student learning can be directly improved (Martinez, 1999). It also ensures that each institution will provide graduates with basic skills that are desired by businesses located in the state. In addition, the exam allows the state to compare student performance prior to enrollment with student performance midway through college. This data offers a measure of accountability to all constituents who want to know what a college education provides. The data can then translate into more support for policy changes or adjustments in financial allocations from the state.

Tennessee is another state that is trying to improve student learning. In 2010, with the announcement that it had received a grant from the federal government to improve education, the Tennessee government passed the Complete College Tennessee Act (CCTA), which ties public funding to outcomes (Tennessee Government, 2010). These outcomes focus on a core curriculum in subjects such as social sciences, arts, history, and math along with skills such as communication, critical thinking, and practical application of theory (Tennessee Higher Education Commission, 2010). Funding is awarded when improvements are made in student learning as defined by annual benchmarks. Although the impact of the CCTA is still unfolding, the state has outlined a general road map for public colleges and universities to follow. Because funding is tied to improvements, Tennessee institutions will become more intentional about their programs and what students are learning on their campuses.

Industry

When the federal and state governments turn their focus to higher education policy, it is often because they have received feedback from industry leaders about a deficiency in the skilled work force (Brown, DesRosier, Peterson, Chida, & Lagier, 2009; Jones, 1995; U.S. Department of Education, 2006). As Carnevale, Gainer, and Meltzer (1990) explained, "From the employers' perspective, the skill of knowing how to learn is cost-effective because it can mitigate the cost of retraining efforts. When workers use efficient learning strategies, they absorb and apply training more quickly, saving their employers money and time" (p. 17). Pascarella and Terenzini (2005) noted, however, that college graduates might not have the skills necessary for the workplace. This observation was reinforced by a national survey of employers conducted by AAC&U (2008). The survey revealed that almost two thirds of employers were dissatisfied with the skills of recent college graduates and that three quarters of employers wanted colleges to place more emphasis on teaching skills such as teamwork in diverse groups, critical thinking and analysis, written and oral communication, information literacy, creativity and innovation, and applying knowledge in real-world environments. In addition, a large study in Canada involving employers, university presidents, faculty, current students, and recent graduates found that students needed four basic competencies:

1. Managing Self: Constantly developing practices and internalizing routines for maximizing one's ability to deal with the uncertainty of an ever-changing environment.
2. Communicating: Interacting effectively with a variety of individuals and groups to facilitate the gathering, integrating, and conveying of information in many forms (for example, verbal, written).
3. Managing People and Tasks: Accomplishing the tasks at hand by planning, organizing, coordinating, and controlling both resources and people.
4. Mobilizing Innovation and Change: Conceptualizing, as well as setting in

motion, ways of initiating and managing change that involve significant depar-
tures from the current mode. (Evers, Rush, and Berdrow, 1998, p. 5)

The authors proposed that these skills are necessary to succeed both in higher education
and in the workplace, both of which are changing due to technology, team-based learning and performance, and accountability to stakeholders (students, parents, customers,
government, etc.) (Evers, Rush, and Berdrow, 1998).

The AAC&U survey also revealed that employers do not have confidence in student
transcripts or data from national surveys to reveal what students have learned from
their college experience. Instead, employers desire individual student assessments based
on observations made by those in direct contact with students (AAC&U, 2008). In
order to obtain direct evidence, employers often look for graduates who have been
involved in student organizations or groups while attending college (Pascarella &
Terenzini, 2005). Research demonstrates that students who have involvement experience can improve skills such as interpersonal communication, leadership abilities, oral
communication, teamwork, data analysis, problem solving, and cognitive development
(Astin, 1993; Kuh, 1995; Pascarella & Terenzini, 2005; Schreiner, 2010). In addition,
student performance in involvement experiences is often directly observed by advisors
and supervisors who can provide recommendation letters or evaluative reports that give
employers a better sense of the individuals who may join their workforce.

Student affairs has a unique opportunity to provide employers with direct evidence
of student learning, yet before carrying out a formal program, it is necessary to better
understand exactly what employers want and need. A number of resources can be
used to uncover this information, such as the Occupational Information Network,
or O*NET, which provides descriptions of jobs and occupations across the nation
(O*NET Resource Center, n.d.) or through professional organizations such as the
National Association of Colleges and Employers.

Another method for obtaining a list of relevant job skills is to use a professional
assessment service that has researched basic skills, developed a variety of ways to
measure these skills, and standardized these methods so they can be used with different
populations to create normed data. Hoover, Giambatista, Sorenson, and Bommer
(2010) used this approach to examine how behavioral skills could be integrated into
a master's degree program in business administration. The main goal of their research
was to respond to criticism that students had the knowledge but not the skills to meet
necessary job responsibilities. In order to determine skill development in their subjects,
the researchers used the basic job-related skills identified by the assessment service,

called the Iliad Assessment Center, to design activities for their subjects to perform outside of the classroom. The purpose of the activities was to reinforce skill development alongside, but separate from, the classroom knowledge the subjects were obtaining. The assessment service administered a pre-test and a post-test in order to track any changes in behavior related to the intervention. At the end of the project, the subjects who participated in the behavioral activities had made significant gains on their assessment tests and had outperformed subjects in a control group.

Although there are financial costs associated with this kind of service, the benefits may outweigh the costs. For instance, skills are clearly defined and activities can be implemented easily and quickly for any student population. In addition, skills can be tailored to fit the mission of any institution or organization as well as to match the desired competencies from employment groups hiring local graduates. The service could also provide ongoing comparisons with other students on a specific campus, as well as groups across the country with similar demographics. Plus, individual students could track and report their scores to potential employers to provide yet another indicator that they have experienced skill growth during college. For busy student affairs professionals, this could be an easy, effective, and efficient tool.

Faculty

Along with understanding what employers want and need, student affairs professionals need to seek feedback from the faculty regarding the appropriate outcomes they need from students. Faculty are closely connected with the career fields served by academic majors, and they understand what knowledge and skills are likely to help their graduates obtain jobs. Faculty also have a thorough understanding of what their curriculum provides to students and what is missing that cannot be covered within the context of a classroom. Tapping into their knowledge can help student affairs create a seamless learning environment by connecting formal and experiential education. Guarasci (2001) explained that it was essential to have a partnership between academic and student affairs to ensure depth of learning. As Arnold and Kuh (1999) noted, "Faculty and student affairs professionals ostensibly are working toward the same ends—preparing a college-educated person to be financially self-sufficient and to live an enlightened, satisfying, socially responsible life after college" (p. 28).

Understanding the faculty perspective is an essential component of creating student learning outcomes, but it is not without obstacles. According to Arnold and Kuh (1999), faculty are primarily focused on the learning that occurs within the classroom and believe that the time spent outside of the classroom should be spent on activities that enrich intellectual development. Some faculty specifically consider involvement in student organizations and other campus activities as unnecessary, and they may not fully understand the depth and breadth of opportunities provided by involvement activities. The researchers also point out that student affairs can become detached from the academic aspect of their institutions, a circumstance that contributes to the faculty view that what student affairs offers is disconnected from what they provide in the classroom (Arnold and Kuh, 1999).

With the faculty's focus on providing the formal education for an institution, it is important for student affairs professionals to take the first step in opening dialogue with faculty. One suggestion is to start the dialogue by engaging faculty in their own academic environment. For example, in 2005 the Division of Student Affairs at Texas A&M University wanted to learn what it could do to support academic units (Student Life Studies, 2005). Faculty members from across the institution and on all levels of the academic career ladder were invited to participate in focus groups. Two primary questions were asked: "What do students need to know, beyond discipline specific knowledge, to be successful in their field?" and "What types of activities or experiences can students engage in outside of class that would help them reinforce the skills and abilities you described?"

The faculty participants noted that they observed growth in students between the freshman and senior years and knew that faculty did not teach that growth in a classroom. Participants also acknowledged that they had to focus on content mastery but that students still had to practice applying that knowledge in other environments because holistic experiences were more appealing to employers. They highlighted specific skills for students to enhance in order to be successful in their careers including group dynamics, communication in all forms, time management, flexibility, resilience, critical thinking, and strategic planning. Participants noted that cocurricular activities such as involvement in student organizations and part-time employment were good opportunities to practice these skills (Student Life Studies, 2005).

In addition to identifying essential skills, the faculty participants recognized areas of improvement for both the faculty and student affairs. Their recommendations for faculty included trying to better understand students' lives outside of the classroom and acknowledging cocurricular activities during classroom discussions so that students would understand the usefulness of applying their knowledge in these settings. For student affairs, the faculty participants observed that students did not always under-stand the value of learning and may not make the connections that are necessary to learning. Their primary recommendation to student affairs was to challenge students to integrate their cocurricular experiences back into academics and to help students make those important connections (Student Life Studies, 2005).

Student Affairs Professionals

In the seminal document *Learning Reconsidered* (Keeling, 2004), student affairs is identified as "integral to the learning process because of the opportunities it provides students to learn through action, contemplation, reflection, and emotional engagement as well as information acquisition" (p. 12). The document goes on to encourage student affairs to provide leadership in defining, assessing, and tracking student learning and offers some criticism for past failings of the profession to focus more intentionally on student learning.

If student affairs is to become more deeply involved in all aspects of student learning, each institution must engage its student affairs staff in identifying potential learning outcomes and competencies that students should be acquiring in the cocurricular environment. Because the field of student affairs encompasses a diverse array of expertise and job responsibilities, large campuses may want to focus initially on collecting feedback from staff members who advise student organizations and/or supervise student employees on a daily basis. These staff members can offer important insights into what they observe students learning, as well as what is missing that should be part of the learning process.

To take an example from one large institution, Texas A&M University developed the Student Leader Learning Outcomes (SLLO) project. Staff members for whom student organization advising was one primary job responsibility were invited to a brainstorming session to answer the question, "Are there common leadership skills that we want student leaders to have at the end of their involvement experience?" (SLLO, n.d.) The goal of this group was to create a set of shared learning outcomes for students who serve in positions of leadership across the institution. The group identified more than 30 skills, including broad areas such as project management, critical thinking, decision making, delegation, diversity, financial management, communication, and time management. After the initial session, staff members formed subcommittees to review relevant literature and research and develop outcomes, assessment rubrics, and accompanying resources for the top five skills identified by the group: project management, communication (oral, written, and interpersonal), groups and teams, critical thinking, and diversity (SLLO, n.d.). Many of the topics developed over time for the SLLO mirror the AAC&U VALUE (Valid Assessment of Learning in Undergraduate Education) Rubrics (Rhodes, 2010).

When the SLLO materials were ready for testing with students, a few staff members volunteered to use them with their student organizations for one year and then report back to the group regarding how SLLO affected the advising experience. One advisor stated, "I become more intentional, but my students become more intentional, which makes my job easier!" Another advisor noted, "They [the skill materials] make my demands for excellence 'universal' rather than just something I cooked up!" Other advisors indicated that the materials "provided a common language" and helped "students become more aware of their strengths and areas for growth" (SLLO, 2008).

At small institutions, the entire division of student affairs may be involved in developing outcomes and competencies. For instance, at Concordia University Irvine (2011), staff members created student learning outcomes to help promote intentional learning throughout all areas of student affairs. They ensured that their outcomes matched the mission of the institution and provided students with concrete examples of how those outcomes might translate into behaviors. For instance, one stated outcome, "Students will grow in responsibility and values through a continual development of a wise mind," included examples such as learning how to ensure personal safety, resolving conflicts without outside assistance, and learning to write and revise a résumé. Having these tools and resources available for all staff members can assist them in promoting learning consistently throughout all cocurricular experiences.

While the actual process of involving student affairs staff members can take many forms, it is critical that all staff members have an opportunity to share their experiences, opinions, and knowledge regarding what students should know or be able to do in the cocurricular environment. Creating a process by which all staff members can contribute will help ensure that all potential learning is explored and that everyone in student affairs can become partners in creating a seamless learning environment.

Current Students and Alumni

Two other essential groups to include in the process of identifying and creating student learning outcomes are those who are and those who have been students at the institution. As Kuh (2004) noted, "It is not possible to determine how well a college or university is achieving its educational purposes" (p. 148) without seeking feedback from these two groups. Other researchers have expressed the same sentiment (Keeling, 2004; Pascarella & Terenzini, 2005).

Suskie (2009) explained that assessments of alumni could identify the impact of their college experiences on career and personal success after graduation. While many colleges and universities may collect feedback from their alumni to help improve the local experience, one researcher set out to discover what the general audience of college alumni might consider important. Zekeri (2004) conducted a study of five different institutions in order to determine the skills and competencies alumni would identify as necessary for their careers. With strong agreement across the institutions represented, the skills participants identified as critical to their career success included communication, problem solving, supervision, critical thinking, and interpersonal relationship skills—all of which align with what employers identify as important. Respondents to other alumni studies not only deal with essential skills but also point to involvement in student organizations as contributing to their skill development and subsequent job success (Kuh, Schuh, & Whitt, 1991) and as providing a catalyst for becoming more engaged in their communities (Johnson, 2004). Researchers emphasize that collecting feedback from alumni is critical if higher education wants to understand the impact of a college education (Cabrera, Weerts, & Zulick, 2005; Sheehan & Granrud, 1995; Wise, Hengstler, & Braskamp, 1981).

While it is easy to identify what is needed for personal and professional success once a career is established, those currently enrolled in college have a harder time understanding what opportunities may be beneficial to them in the future. Current students tend to focus on the formal academic curriculum and do not easily identify the opportunities that are available to them for learning outside the classroom or across campus (Arnold & Kuh, 1999). They may view the cocurriculum only through the lens of their social environment and may need assistance connecting seemingly unrelated activities back to their classroom experiences and professional goals (Keeling, 2004).

Evers, Rush, and Berdrow (1998) explained that it is essential that students lead their own learning and identify their strengths and areas for growth, a call that is echoed by other researchers (Brown, DesRosier, Peterson, Chida, & Lagier, 2009; Huba & Freed, 2000; Schreiner, 2010). Once students understand what they need to develop, they are better equipped to identify development opportunities. The power of leading students to reflect on their learning is illustrated in an example from Texas A&M University highlighted earlier in the section on student affairs professionals.

For the SLLO project, student organization advisors and supervisors worked with their student leaders/employees on specific skills that could be addressed through organizational responsibilities. Student leaders learned from their advisors what detailed skills could help them improve larger skill sets. For instance, since many student organizations plan events, one large skill was event planning. However, several components work together to enhance the skill of event planning. These components include areas such as financial management, delegation, and effective meeting management (SLLO, 2009). The resource materials developed for the SLLO project helped the advisors discuss all potential areas of learning with their student leaders, and, in turn, the student leaders could identify what areas they could individually emphasize during the year. Advisors and student leaders revisited individual and group progress on the identified skills a few times during an academic calendar year, including at the beginning, midpoint, and end of the school year. Students and the leadership team received feedback from the advisors, and in some instances from fellow students, regarding how skills were progressing and what might still need to be addressed.

At the end of the school year, focus groups were conducted with the student leaders who used the SLLO materials in order to gain a greater understanding of how the materials and process affected them. Below is a sample of what students learned through participating in the SLLO project for one school year (SLLO, 2009).

- "This program really provided almost like benchmarks that I can look at and say, through this program or through all of [my organization] as a whole, I've really gained these skills." –Freshman leadership group executive
- "It is really hard to remember that we're here to try to improve as leaders and as an organization, not just to keep everything in the air at the same time. Because if I'm not forced to do stuff like that I'm just going to concentrate on just exactly what I have to do for next week, the next month, for the next meeting, for the next event." –Class Council officer
- "I kind of stopped assuming that everybody knew everything, how to do everything, and started helping others." –Student employee working with Late Night Program

It should be noted that the students can take on a variety of roles and gain different benefits from the process. For example, some of the quotes offered above came from students who were paid employees of a student union unit. Although some student employees may perform such basic office tasks as answering the phone and making copies, student affairs often has student employees that are asked to take on greater responsibilities, such as managing a facility or coordinating the needs of a residence hall floor. When job responsibilities require additional skills from students, student learning outcomes may be beneficial to both student employees and those who supervise them.

The University of Rhode Island (2006) created student employee outcomes along with a rubric to measure progress in each area. The outcomes include explaining the mission of the organization and the individual student employee's role within it, solving work-related problems, working independently, having good time management skills, presenting an appropriate personal image while at work, maintaining confidentiality, working collaboratively with others, and using feedback constructively. The rubric that accompanies the explanation of outcomes breaks down each outcome into performance measures so that students can clearly see what is expected of them. Including learning outcomes in the regular performance review process can help students focus on skills outside of the specific job requirements and develop in a more intentional manner.

Conclusions and Recommendations

In their Documenting Effective Educational Practices study, Kuh, Kinzie, Schuh, and Whitt (2005) found that institutions that successfully focus on student learning do so throughout the campus. For instance, student affairs staff design cocurricular opportunities to complement the educational goals of the campus rather than organizing activities that may detract from the intellectual environment. Using these high-performing institutions as a foundation, the authors recommended that colleges and universities shape all learning opportunities so that students understand them better and are more motivated to become active participants. Other researchers advocated sharing expectations for learning and providing feedback on performance so students can increase their likelihood of engagement and success in learning (Huba & Freed, 2000; Schreiner, 2010). As Pascarella and Terenzini (2005) noted, "Other things being equal, the more the student is psychologically engaged in activities and tasks that reinforce and extend the formal academic experience, the more he or she will learn" (p. 119).

The purpose of this chapter was to review a variety of sources that can provide essential feedback on what students should learn in the college environment. It is also important to highlight the different steps that student affairs professionals should take to create a culture of learning in the cocurricular environment that not only helps students but also aligns with the demands of the modern university. Below are some suggested phases for student affairs professionals to consider in identifying and developing appropriate student learning outcomes.

Ask Big-picture Questions and Create Possible Answers

As a starting point for identifying appropriate student learning goals, a number of important questions should be considered. Bresciani, Zelna, and Anderson (2004) provided several questions to start the planning process, such as: What should students know or be able to do at the end of their cocurricular experience? How do these cocurricular experiences contribute to the academic environment? Who benefits from these experiences, and how do they benefit? How is learning promoted within these experiences? How are connections made between cocurricular experiences and classroom learning? What kind of evaluations and feedback do students receive? Attempting to create reasonable responses to these questions can help student affairs staff focus on the underlying learning needs of students and how they can be addressed in various contexts.

Align Student Learning Outcomes with Institutional Statements

When student learning outcomes are developed, verify that they match the stated institutional mission, vision, values, and goals. Aligning outcomes with the broader institutional purpose will help student affairs build a student learning program that can be supported throughout the campus rather than being seen as detracting from the academic mission.

Examine What Constituents Want or Need

As noted in this chapter, important constituents include the federal and state governments, accrediting bodies for the institution as a whole and for specific academic disciplines, relevant professional associations, employers who hire or could potentially hire the institution's graduates, alumni, faculty, current students, and other student affairs professionals on campus. Collecting this data using a variety of methods, from conducting surveys to interviewing individuals to reviewing materials posted on official websites, will help student affairs staff understand what constituents might need and want from cocurricular experiences.

Seek Additional Information from Other Areas of Campus

Seeking feedback from constituents is vital to the development of student learning outcomes; however, other units at the institution may have useful information that can be incorporated into the process. For example, campus career centers typically have some kind of feedback from employers regarding what they are looking for in graduates, how many students they hire each year, and for what positions they hire. The financial aid office may track how many students are employed on campus and where they are employed. Checking with these offices on the information they may have about student learning and skill development can help solidify the foundation being created for the outcomes process.

Identify Areas of Repetition

Once feedback is collected from all constituents and resource areas, pay special attention to any competencies or skills that are identified multiple times. These areas may need to be the first ones developed as student learning outcomes, with accompanying opportunities identified both in and out of the classroom. Starting with the most important competencies and skills can help obtain needed support from constituents.

Delve More Deeply Into Identified Competencies and Skills

Seeking feedback from all constituents can generate a comprehensive list of competencies and skills. However, the list might be too broad to be effective. For instance, one skill that appeared several times in this chapter was communication. There is an entire field of study concerning communication, as well as a variety of skills. What is meant by communication? Does it refer to writing skills, presentation skills, marketing skills, or something else? If written communication is pinpointed as an important skill for the institution's graduates, what area of written communication should be the focus—grammar, sentence structure, spelling, or something more advanced? By delving more deeply into the initially identified competencies and skills, learning outcomes can be better defined and more useful to both student affairs staff and students.

Generate a List of Existing Cocurricular Opportunities

Once learning outcomes are developed and verified as important to constituents and to the institution, student affairs then should identify all existing opportunities outside of the classroom that could help students develop these skills. By focusing on existing activities, student affairs recognizes the valuable contributions of current opportunities and becomes more intentional about how these opportunities are presented and managed.

Use Existing Resources

A number of useful resources are available to anyone interested in developing student learning outcomes. For instance, the National Institute for Learning Outcomes Assessment (NILOA) developed a "Transparency Framework" that offers a variety of resources institutions can use for student learning, such as national tests that measure learning, examples of curriculum mapping, and social communication networks such as listservs and blogs that can address specific issues (NILOA, 2011). The AAC&U VALUE Rubrics (2007) provide greater detail for the competencies identified as essential for student learning at a variety of higher education institutions. The rubrics are a good starting point and can easily be adapted to the needs of a specific campus. Finally, there is a variety of good books that guide readers through every step of developing student learning outcomes (e.g., Bresciani, Zelna, & Anderson, 2004; Suskie, 2009).

It is important to keep in mind that student learning is a continuous process and that the steps outlined above should be revisited periodically to ensure that the big questions are still relevant, constituents have an opportunity to provide updated feedback, new data can be reviewed, skills can be refined, new institutional endeavors can be incorporated, and opportunities can be reassessed for appropriate alignment. This process can take years. The key is to start somewhere and create a realistic plan that keeps the process moving forward. It may be necessary to start with just one student and have him or her develop a learning plan for an upcoming semester or quarter. While it may not seem like a big step, this kind of activity can provide practice for engaging students in the learning process and can offer student affairs professionals important insight into what future exploration may be needed. If even one student leader is receptive and agrees to participate in an intentional learning process, that student can assist in motivating other students. Helping individual students identify what they want to improve and how the advisor can aid them in that process throughout the year will then ignite the student's desire to learn. Then the benefits of individual growth will be shared among peers who will be receptive to the process in subsequent years.

Questions for Reflection

1. What should students know or be able to do when they complete cocurricular activities offered by the institution?
2. How do the student learning outcomes align with institution statements such as mission, vision, and goals?
3. Do the student learning outcomes meet the expectations of institution constituents?
4. Do other campus units have data that can inform the creation, refinement, or implementation of student learning outcomes?
5. Are the student learning outcomes fully defined with specific behaviors expected from students?
6. How do the student learning outcomes align with existing cocurricular opportunities?

References

ABET. (2010). About ABET. Retrieved from http://www.abet.org

American College Personnel Association (ACPA). (1996). *Student learning imperative: Implications for student affairs.* Retrieved from http://www.acpa.nche.edu/sli/sli.htm

American College Personnel Association (ACPA) & National Association of Student Personnel Administrators (NASPA), Joint Task Force on Professional Competencies and Standards. (2010). *ACPA/NASPA professional competency areas for student affairs practitioners.* Retrieved from http://www.naspa.org/programs/prodev/ACPA-NASPA%20Professional%20Competency%20Areas-Preliminary%20Version.pdf

Arnold, A., & Kuh, G. D. (1999). What matters in undergraduate education? Mental models, student learning, and student affairs. In E. J. Whitt (Ed.), *Student learning as student affairs work* (pp. 11–34). Washington, DC: National Association of Student Personnel Administrators.

Association of American Colleges and Universities (AAC&U). (2007). *College learning for the new global century.* Retrieved from http://www.aacu.org/leap/documents/GlobalCentury_ExecSum_3.pdf

Association of American Colleges and Universities (AAC&U). (2008). VALUE: Valid assessment of learning in undergraduate education. Retrieved from http://www.aacu.org/value/index.cfm

Association of Fraternity/Sorority Advisors. (2009). Assessment. Retrieved from http://www.fraternityadvisors.org/KnowledgeCenter/Assessment.aspx

Astin, A. (1993). *What matters in college? Four critical years revisited.* San Francisco, CA: Jossey-Bass.

Bresciani, M. J., Zelna, C. L., & Anderson, J. A. (2004). *Assessing student learning and development: A handbook for practitioners.* Washington, DC: National Association of Student Personnel Administrators.

Brown, G., DesRosier, T., Peterson, N., Chida, M., & Lagier, R. (2009). Engaging employers in assessment. *About Campus, 14*(5), 5–14.

Cabrera, A. F., Weerts, D. J., & Zulick, B. J. (2005). Making an impact with alumni surveys. In D. J. Weerts & J. Vidal (Eds.), *Special issue: Enhancing alumni research: European and American perspectives* (New directions for institutional research, no. 126, pp. 5–17). San Francisco, CA: Jossey-Bass.

Carnevale, A. P., Gainer, L. J., & Meltzer, A. S. (1990). *Workplace basics: The essential skills employers want.* San Francisco, CA: Jossey-Bass.

Cohen, A. M. (1998). *The shaping of American higher education: Emergence and growth of the contemporary system.* San Francisco, CA: Jossey-Bass.

Concordia University Irvine. (2011). Student outcomes. Retrieved from http://www. cui.edu/studentlife/residential-education-services/index.aspx?id=20680

Council for the Advancement of Standards in Higher Education (CAS). (2010). Professional services. Retrieved from http://www.cas.edu/index.php/index.php/index.php

Evers, F. T., Rush, J. C., & Berdrow, I. (1998). *The bases of competence: Skills for lifelong learning and employability.* San Francisco, CA: Jossey-Bass.

Guarasci, R. (2001). Recentering learning: An interdisciplinary approach to academic and student affairs. In A. Kezar, D. J. Hirsch, & C. Burack (Eds.), *Special issue: Understanding the role of academic and student affairs collaboration in creating a successful learning environment* (New directions for higher education, no. 116, pp. 101–110). San Francisco, CA: Jossey-Bass.

Hoover, J. D., Giambatista, R. C., Sorenson, R. L., & Bommer, W. H. (2010). Assessing the effectiveness of whole person learning pedagogy in skill acquisition. *Academy of Management Learning & Education, 9*(2), 192–203.

Huba, M. E., & Freed, J. E. (2000). *Learner-centered assessment on college campuses: Shifting the focus from teaching to learning.* Needham Heights, MA: Allyn & Bacon.

Johnson, D. I. (2004). Relationships between college experiences and alumni participation in the community. *The Review of Higher Education, 27*(2), 169–185.

Jones, E. A. (1995). *National assessment of college student learning: Identifying college graduates' essential skills in writing, speech and listening, and critical thinking.* Washington, DC: National Center for Education Statistics.

Keeling, R. P. (Ed.). (2004). *Learning reconsidered: A campus-wide focus on the student experience.* Washington, DC: American College Personnel Association and National Association of Student Personnel Administrators.

Keeling, R. P., Wall, A. F., Underhile, R., & Dungy, G. J. (2008). *Assessment reconsidered: Institutional effectiveness for student success.* Washington, DC: American College Personnel Association and National Association of Student Personnel Administrators.

Kuh, G. D. (1995). The other curriculum: Out-of-class experiences associated with student learning and personal development. *The Journal of Higher Education, 66*(2), 123–155.

Kuh, G. D. (2004). Imagine asking the client: Using student and alumni surveys for accountability in higher education. In J. C. Burke (Ed.), *Achieving accountability in higher education: Balancing public, academic, and market demands* (pp. 148–172). San Francisco, CA: Jossey-Bass.

Kuh, G., & Ikenberry, S. (2009). *More than you think, less than we need: Learning outcomes assessment in American higher education.* Urbana, IL: University of Illinois and Indiana University, National Institute for Learning Outcomes Assessment.

Kuh, G. D., Kinzie, J., Schuh, J. H., & Whitt, E. J. (2005). *Student success in college: Creating conditions that matter.* San Francisco, CA: Jossey-Bass.

Kuh, G. D., Schuh, J. H., & Whitt, E. J. (1991). *Involving colleges: Successful approaches to fostering student learning and development outside the classroom.* San Francisco, CA: Jossey-Bass.

Martinez, M. C. (1999, June). *South Dakota: Developing policy-driven change in higher education.* Retrieved from http://www.highereducation.org/reports/dakota/dakota.pdf

Miami Dade College. (n.d.a). About MDC. Retrieved from http://www.mdc.edu/main/about/mission_vision.aspx

Miami Dade College. (n.d.b). Learning outcomes at MDC. Retrieved from http://www.mdc.edu/learningoutcomes/about_new.aspx

Middaugh, M. F. (2010). *Planning and assessment in higher education.* San Francisco, CA: Jossey-Bass.

National Institute for Learning Outcomes Assessment (NILOA). (2011). Transparency Framework. Retrieved from http://www.learningoutcomesassessment.org/TransparencyFramework.htm

O*NET Resource Center. (n.d.). About O*NET. Retrieved from http://www.onetcenter.org/overview.html

Pascarella, E. T., & Terenzini, P. T. (2005). *How college affects students: A third decade of research*. San Francisco, CA: Jossey-Bass.

Rhodes, T. (Ed.). (2010). *Assessing outcomes and improving achievement: Tips and tools for using rubrics*. Washington, DC: Association of American Colleges and Universities.

Rudolph, F. (1990). *The American college and university: A history*. Athens, GA: The University of Georgia Press.

Schreiner, L. A. (2010). The "thriving quotient": A new vision for student success. *About Campus, 15*(2), 2–10.

Sheehan, E. P., & Granrud, C. E. (1995). Assessment of student outcomes: Evaluating an undergraduate psychology program. *Journal of Instructional Psychology, 22*, 366–372.

Sheldon, H. D. (1901). *The history and pedagogy of American student societies*. Worcester, MA: Clark University.

South Dakota Board of Regents. (n.d.). *Regental proficiency examination administration guidelines*. Retrieved from http://www.sdbor.edu/services/academics/AAC/documents/prof_exam_guidelines.pdf

Student Leader Learning Outcomes (SLLO). (n.d.). Executive summary revised. Retrieved from http://sllo.tamu.edu/historical-documents

Student Life Studies. (2005). [Faculty focus groups]. Unpublished raw data.

Student Leader Learning Outcomes (SLLO). (2008). [Advisor focus groups]. Unpublished raw data.

Student Leader Learning Outcomes (SLLO). (2009). [Student focus groups]. Unpublished raw data.

Suskie, L. (2009). *Assessing student learning: A common sense approach* (2nd ed.). San Francisco, CA: Jossey-Bass.

Tennessee Government. (2010, January 26). Bredesen signs landmark education bills into law. Retrieved from http://news.tn.gov/node/4490

Tennessee Higher Education Commission. (2010). The public agenda for Tennessee higher education 2010–2015. Retrieved from http://www.tn.gov/thec/complete_college_tn

U.S. Department of Education. (2006). *A test of leadership: Charting the future of U.S. higher education.* Washington, DC: Author.

U. S. Department of Labor. (1991, June). *What work requires of schools: A SCANS report for America 2000.* Washington, DC: Department of Labor, The Secretary's Commission on Achieving Necessary Skills.

University of Rhode Island. (2006). Assessment of learning for URI student affairs employees. Retrieved from http://www.uri.edu.assessment/media/public/page_files/uri/outcomes/student/tools/SELOs_Survey_pdf%5B1%5D.doc.pdf

Upcraft, M. L., & Schuh, J. H. (1996). *Assessment in student affairs: A guide for practitioners.* San Francisco, CA: Jossey-Bass.

White House. (n.d.). Education. Retrieved from http://www.whitehouse.gov/issues/education

Whitt, E. J. (2006). Are all your educators educating? *About Campus, 10*(6), 2–9.

Wise, S. L., Hengstler, D. D., & Braskamp, L. A. (1981). Alumni ratings as an indicator of departmental quality. *Journal of Educational Psychology, 75,* 71–77.

Zekeri, A. A. (2004). College curriculum competencies and skills former students found essential to their careers. *College Student Journal, 38*(3), 412–422.

CHAPTER 4

ASSESSING AND DOCUMENTING STUDENT LEARNING

How Do We Do It?

Matt Starcke and Adrien DeLoach

At the crux of any educational experience is the simple question, "Did the students learn what we wanted them to?" Before answering this, however, we must step back and ask ourselves, "What do we want students to learn?" This chapter focuses primarily on various assessment tools. However, the critical question that must be asked before assessment takes place is "What, exactly, is being assessed?" Key to this process is developing clear and measurable learning outcomes.

Put simply, learning outcomes describe what students will know or be able to do after participating in a class, activity, or program (Huba & Freed, 2000; Suskie, 2009). Unlike satisfaction outcomes, learning outcomes should capture what students will gain from an experience rather than the experience itself (Huba & Freed, 2000). While it may be tempting to ask participants, "What did you like about today's activity?" or "What would you change to make this program more enjoyable?" neither question defines nor measures the impact of the experience on the participant.

Also, learning outcomes provide purpose for activities and tell participants what objectives the instructor or facilitator finds important (Huba & Freed, 2000). For participants, the effect is twofold. First, they better understand the context in which lessons or activities take place. Second, by clearly stating the outcomes in advance of the experience, the facilitator imparts a level of significance to the forthcoming experience. Ultimately, instead of wondering, "Why are we doing this?" students are encouraged to deliberately connect their experience to stated course or program goals. Ideally, students will begin to make holistic meaning of their college experiences as those experiences build upon each other.

Of course, it would be possible for administrators to develop lengthy lists of learning outcomes for each program. However, Suskie (2009) suggested identifying and defining only the primary goals of a program or course when writing learning outcomes. For example, students participating in a personal values workshop may be asked to document their beliefs, discuss them in small groups, and then participate in a larger discussion. While it is plausible these students may practice and improve their writing and interpersonal communication skills, these were probably not the intended outcomes of the event. Instead, the program designer would be likely to focus stated outcomes around each participant's ability to identify and discuss his or her respective values.

If the goal of documenting learning outcomes is to be able to measure them and then improve upon performance, the way each outcome is written is important. Effective learning outcomes rely on action words indicative of specific behaviors (Suskie, 2009). In a personal values workshop, a clearly stated outcome might read, "Participants will be able to define the term 'value.'" Contrast this outcome with "Participants will understand the term 'value,'" and the difference is evident. In the first example, an administrator could easily measure whether or not each student could define "value" following the program; it is more performance oriented. In the second statement, however, the term "understand" is vague and open to interpretation by each participant.

Ultimately, learning outcomes "form the basis of assessment at the course, program, and institutional levels" (Huba & Freed, 2000, p. 94). With clear, measurable learning outcomes established, administrators must then decide how best to measure success in achieving these goals. Even so, "while progress is being made in identifying common learning outcomes across institutions and even across countries, development of measures to assess student achievement of these outcomes is in its infancy" (Banta, Griffin, Flateby, & Kahn, 2009, p. 5).

This chapter will explore several tools that are available to student affairs professionals to measure the learning that students are experiencing through their involvement in campus activities and student employment. These tools include rubrics, surveys, reflections, interviews and focus groups, portfolios, pre- and post-tests, and learning contracts.

Rubrics

The rubric is a rather effective tool in gauging the development of student leaders. Suskie (2009) tells us that a rubric is a "scoring guide: a list or chart that describes the criteria that you . . . will use to evaluate or grade completed assignments" (p. 137). It details "acceptable or unacceptable levels of performance" (Stevens & Levi, 2005, p. 3). When applied to campus activities, rubrics enable a student advisor or employer to use a matrix that may include a variety of levels denoting improved performance, skills, or comprehension in a given area. Typically, students navigate through a particular set of criteria and/or dimensions, achieving prescribed levels of attainment along the way. Detailed descriptions of these stages of accomplishment allow students to monitor the progress of their skill and understanding in each area of development (Allen & Tanner, 2006).

Why would a student affairs professional want to use a rubric to document student learning? It is simple: Rubrics are an easy way to evaluate a student's performance on a given task. In addition to this, the rubric itself provides a springboard from which the advisor/supervisor can initiate a conversation with and give timely feedback to the student (Stevens & Levi, 2005). Rubrics are beneficial when used with students individually, particularly if the interaction occurs over a period of time. Banta, Griffin, Flateby, and Kahn (2009) also suggested that rubrics can be used to communicate expectations and engage students in a peer review process so that the emphasis is not always on the hierarchical relationship. Therefore, rubrics are an easy way to provide structured feedback to individual students so they can improve student learning and success throughout their college experience.

After deciding a rubric is the right method, it is necessary to decide which type of rubric to use. For use with student leaders and employees, advisors and supervisors should consider choosing either analytical or holistic models. Analytical rubrics are more detailed in criteria, spanning numerous levels of accomplishment. They often imply that there is a "best match" associated with the expectations given and they must meet objectives in each specific area. Holistic rubrics use a more general approach in describing categories for quality and or mastery levels (Luft, 1999). Additionally, in a holistic rubric, the criteria are less specific and/or "lumped together" when distinguishing progress or development (Allen & Tanner, 2006).

Rubrics are used to articulate clear standards or expectations to students; guide and enhance student leader performance; formulate criteria for progress and accomplishments (Allen & Tanner, 2006); and provide a tool for student feedback in achieving learning outcomes (Muirhead, 2002). Although commonly used in the K–12 educational environment (Luft, 1999), the idea of implementing rubrics has been found to be attractive at institutions of higher education as well (Allen & Tanner, 2006). Incorporating rubrics for student organization leaders and student employees can prove beneficial in several ways. Rubrics can promote reflective practice and motivate advisors to give clear instructions and relate directly to learning objectives. Rubrics can assist advisors and supervisors in intentionally developing their students. Rubrics also encourage students to challenge conventional strategies for accomplishing their organizational mission, examine their individual behavior as group members, and enhance their knowledge about their particular role within the organization (Luft, 1999).

According to conventional practice, there are five key elements in constructing an effective rubric. In the realm of student organizational leadership and working with student employees, these components may be levels of mastery, dimensions of quality, organizational groupings, commentaries, and descriptions of consequences (Muirhead, 2002). These elements can be slightly modified in order to better apply to individual student leaders and employees. Alternative terms for rubric components could include levels of performance, dimensions of comprehension, organizational aptitude, commentaries, and enlightenments.

Levels of performance denote in what terms leadership proficiency will be described. For example, on the rubric itself, students may be categorized as novice, intermediate, or advanced. A rubric has been provided at the end of this chapter for your reference (see Appendix A). This rubric, developed by the Student Leader Learning Outcomes project team at Texas A&M University, specifically addresses "teams and groups" and is based on Tuckman and Jensen's Model of Group Development (1977) (see Chapter 5 for more information). Stevens and Levi (2005) suggested using emerging, progressing, partial mastery, and mastery as active, positive terms, although they provide many different options to fit a variety of situations. Dimensions of comprehension address student leader awareness on a variety of levels, and organizational aptitude concerns how quickly or easily students acquire teamwork and/or critical thinking skills. Leadership abilities and potential can be measured to determine how well each student will fit into his or her particular role within the organization. Commentaries refer to any detailed descriptions made by the advisor, supervisor, or rubric administrator that define each student's developmental progress. These remarks can be categorized to denote what may be considered outstanding, average, or below standard. Enlightenments are detailed descriptions of lessons that students learned as a result of their unique leadership experiences. The purpose of these accounts is to provide students with practical applications to the real world (Muirhead, 2002).

Using different terms, Stevens and Levi (2005) described the components of a rubric as task description, scale, dimensions, and descriptions of dimensions. The task description can be the specific assignment, the overall behavior, or the outcomes expected. The scale is the rating of performance using descriptors (e.g., high, medium, low), numbers, or grades. The dimensions clarify components of the performance. For example, if you are rating how effectively the president of a student organization runs a meeting, you might evaluate whether the agenda was created and sent out ahead of time, whether the meeting started and ended on time, how the president maintained order, and how well the president communicated with the other officers and members. The descriptions of dimensions provide specific examples of what constitutes performance at each level.

Rubrics are used extensively in classrooms throughout higher education, but they are less common in the cocurricular environment and take time to develop initially. As you start to create your rubric, it makes sense to ask a faculty colleague to share one that he or she has used to grade assignments. Another way to go about researching rubrics is to conduct a simple online search, as many colleges require their faculty to post rubrics. The Association of American Colleges and Universities created VALUE (Valid Assessment of Learning in Undergraduate Education) Rubrics that can be adapted for student affairs work. Fifteen total rubrics were developed around the topics of critical thinking; inquiry and analysis; reading; written communication; oral communication; creative thinking; teamwork; problem solving; quantitative literacy; information literacy; civic knowledge and engagement; intercultural knowledge and competence; ethical reasoning; integrative and applied learning; and foundations and skills for lifelong learning (Rhodes, 2010).

The benefits of using rubrics allow for consistent assessment of learning outcomes, specify behavior expectations, and provide an opportunity for reflection and goal setting. Quality rubrics take some time to develop and test before fully implementing. For best results they should be executed several times over the course of an experience, and advisors and supervisors need to commit the time and effort to work with individual students on their performance.

Surveys

Perhaps one of the most popular methods of collecting data is to conduct a survey. This section reviews key aspects of surveys, but many books and articles have been written on the subject that provide more in-depth descriptions. Surveys are "systematic efforts to collect information about people by asking them to respond to specific questions about their backgrounds, experiences, plans, opinions, and attitudes" (Suskie, 2009, p. 198). Surveys can be a combination of questions that encourage student leaders to reflect on their leadership experiences. This process can be accomplished through the Internet, over the telephone, on paper, or in person. As they apply to campus activity-based student learning, surveys are typically associated with measuring programming satisfaction and/or effectiveness. In relation to student involvement or employment, surveys can be used to evaluate how and why students learn, set objectives, and determine whether or not objectives have been achieved, as well as to measure student staff satisfaction (Beam, 2005).

Surveys such as the National Survey of Student Engagement or the Multi-Institutional Study of Leadership can be purchased to provide local as well as comparative information. However, developing an instrument for your own campus may be worthwhile. When designing a survey, consider first the type of information needs to be gathered and the best way to go about acquiring it. Ask yourself: "What do I need to know and how can the results be used?" (Beam, 2005, p. 2). According to Beam, there are seven essential steps in designing every survey: planning, content, layout formatting, survey distribution, data collection and processing, data analysis, and reporting the results. These steps overlap and collectively make up three larger, overarching phases. Phase 1 consists of the first three steps in sequence, Phase 2 consists of the next two steps, and Phase 3 consists of the last two steps (Beam, 2005).

The very first step in planning any assessment is to clarify why the research is being conducted. Advisors and supervisors should create a survey purpose statement, making sure it matches the objectives of the student learning outcomes they are working with (Beam, 2005). It is also good practice to articulate the purpose statement when administering the questionnaire to students and soliciting participation (Suskie, 2009). After the initial planning comes developing the content of the assessment. The survey should be focused and simple, rather than "long and arduous" (Suskie, 2004, p. 238). Questions must be clear, concise, and tailored so that respondents are able to answer each one, interpreting them the same way that other members of their cohort would. Questions should also have a direct relation to the objectives of the survey, as well as provide answers to exactly what information is needed (Beam, 2005). According to Suskie (2009), it is a good idea to pilot the survey with a sample group before distribution. This will allow you to examine the length of the instrument and clarity of questions and even to gather feedback from a smaller sample of individuals before you release the survey to your intended audience.

In developing questions for a survey, there are numerous alternatives to choose from. Some commonly used formats are multiple choice, check lists, ranking, rating scales, and open-ended or fill-in-the-blank, among others (Beam, 2005). Each solicits a specific response and has certain limitations. For instance, multiple-choice alternatives are frequently used because they can be responded to and tallied quickly. Their down side is that survey participants can only choose from the options that are available (Suskie, 2009). Rankings, ratings such as Likert scales, and check lists all fall into this category and are often synonymous with quantitative assessment. In contrast, open-ended alternatives allow for much richer and elaborate data collection. These methods of questioning provide valuable insights to complement the closed-ended responses (Beam, 2005).

Before deciding how to lay out your survey, there are a few items of professionalism that must be addressed. Provide students or participants with an opening statement explaining the purpose of the research and how the collected data will be used, as well as any benefits associated with their participation. You can provide a disclaimer of confidentiality and note how long the assessment will take to complete (Beam, 2005). Prior to administering the survey, consider offering participants a summary of the findings after the final analysis has been completed. This would show the students that their efforts could make a difference (Suskie, 2009).

There are a variety of survey layouts to choose from. The purpose of the survey will often determine the format. For instance, if an advisor is seeking quantitative data that may lead to major decisions affecting a large student population, then he or she may want to administer some form of questionnaire that results in the credibility of having responses from a critical mass of students. Thorough research and an extensive range of participants promotes greater confidence in the findings upon presentation to any reviewers (Suskie, 2009). Mailed, electronic, and in-person questionnaires and perhaps even telephone interviews would all work well for this type of data collection. The exchange is efficient as long as participants are allowed to make brief responses or simple ratings about their views and experiences. However, for lengthier questions and or complex rating scales, paper or electronic (web-based) surveys may prove more effective (Suskie, 2009). Long and complex surveys generally have a lower response rate, which decreases credibility.

Once the survey design and layout are complete, a target audience or population must be identified. Who has the information you need? Student leaders, employees, organization members, the general student body? How can you best reach them? Due to the millennial generation's knack for using technology as a viable communication device, web-based/mobile device surveys may also be successful tools. Student organization advisors and student employee supervisors have a captive audience in their student leaders, but they also have access to accurate contact information such as e-mail addresses for electronic questionnaire distribution and follow up. Follow-up contact, or touching base with survey participants, is the single best strategy for maximizing response rate. In fact, Suskie (2009) reported that follow up can almost double the response rate.

Costs associated with surveys must be carefully weighed against benefits, as they could impose a series of restrictions on the types of assessments used, as well as determining how data can be distributed and/or collected. Fortunately, technology has come a long way to help. Online survey systems can be free or low cost for simple assessments. Scanning technology has improved over time, although those systems still require the purchase of some hardware and software. Without scanning technology, the cost of personnel for data entry and the use of a massive quantity of paper must be included.

After all survey responses have been collected, it is time to start data analysis. Some of the collected information will be statistical and some more qualitative. It is necessary to focus on the representation of the participant group as a whole through the data. There may be extreme responses, correlations or associations between responses, or perhaps failure to respond at all. Ultimately, advisors and supervisors are encouraged to conduct their own data analysis, engage graduate students interested in the topic, use their respective institutional research offices or, when available, use an in-house student affairs assessment staff (Beam, 2005).

In reporting the results and using the collected data, there is often a conundrum regarding what to do with the information. Ideally, before beginning a student learning outcomes project using a survey, you have already considered how you are going to report the information, who needs the information and in what format, how you will respond to negative responses, and what changes will or can be made based on the results.

Reflection

Another method for assessing student learning is reflection. This type of qualitative feedback can be used to measure attitudes, skills, and knowledge. It involves encouraging students to internalize and articulate exactly what lessons they have learned, in what areas they have developed, and perhaps even why those experiences made such an impact. Along with evaluating performance, reflection tools may also be used to gauge student satisfaction (Suskie, 2009).

Reflection helps develop metacognition and synthesis skills, corroborate quantitative student learning assessment, and provide quick and efficient information that can be used for a variety of reasons. The main purpose for using the reflection method is to increase learning aptitude by helping students identify the ways in which they learn best as well as pulling together a compilation of lessons for a holistic perspective of learning. Having students think about how they may have improved in skills or knowledge at the end of a learning experience and then having them document those accounts adds to their metacognitive development. And much like surveys, reflective feedback provides the type of precious insight that supports quantitative data and can be collected from short question or brief paragraph responses (Suskie, 2009).

Reflection activities can also be incorporated in collaboration with portfolios (Suskie, 2009), which are examined later in this chapter. By asking students at the beginning of a program to think about what they expect to learn and then comparing those responses to their thoughts at the end of the program about what they actually learned, the students gain a sense of how much they have grown in the process. Having students assess their awareness in developing as leaders not only enhances skills but also positively influences attitudes (Suskie, 2009).

A couple of quick and easy ways to implement reflection with your students is through minute papers and short questions. Minute papers call for students to respond in no more than a sentence to one or two questions in approximately two minutes (Suskie, 2009). Questions may be structured along the following lines:

- What is something new that you learned from this experience?
- What is something old that you interpreted in a new way?
- Specifically, what about this experience helped you learn more effectively? Or what might have hindered your learning?
- What elements can you apply to your personal or academic experiences?

Short questions or prompts can also be effective if implemented properly. They can either be disseminated by themselves or presented as part of a survey. And they must only be used if the question is interesting enough for students to respond. If not, the question may go unanswered or deter respondents from completing the survey. Journals are also an efficient development method. Because they assist students by teaching repetition, journals enhance written communication, behavior awareness, and critical thinking skills (Suskie, 2009).

A more detailed approach to reflection called "articulated learnings" consists of a series of written paragraphs done in a three-step process focusing on specific learning objectives. These categories are curriculum oriented, experiential learning, and personal areas of development. Students are encouraged by a peer guide or "reflection leader" to write their experiential responses throughout several stages. Instructors or advisors also offer feedback to participating students, who in turn ultimately submit a "raw, revised, and final" articulated learning document or video (Ash, Clayton, & Atkinson, 2005).

Baxter Magolda and King (2008) described a process for academic advisors to use to encourage students to make meaning through reflection. The model can be adapted to student affairs staff who advise or supervise. The first step is getting acquainted and building rapport. This allows students to talk about their expectations, early experiences, and backgrounds. The next step, encouraging reflection about important experiences, asks students to think about and interpret defining moments, challenges, successes, decision making, and stresses. The third step, encouraging interpretation of these reflections, challenges students to make sense of what they have shared and how it has affected them. The conversation may be about values and beliefs, working with others, personal development, or future decisions. As each conversation concludes, thank students for sharing their stories and encourage them to continue reflection.

There are a few problems with using reflection as an assessment tool. Because self-reflection is so heavily centered around an individual experience, it may become difficult to validate that experience in relation to the rest of the data collected. Therefore, there may not be an accurate way to grade or score this type of feedback (Suskie, 2009). Also, due to their emotive nature, it is easy to either stifle true attitudes or sway students into thinking that they should respond in ways that we might want them to respond. As with the articulated learnings approach, you must be extremely careful not to impose expectations of what reflective responses will be, which could force responses toward the learning objectives (Ash, Clayton, & Atkinson, 2005). Finally, if implementation is not done in a brief or concise fashion, as is the case with short questions and minute papers, students may offer lackluster responses or simply avoid these open-ended items altogether (Suskie, 2009). To combat that problem, you might create one online question for students to answer at their convenience, using various types of questions and also ensuring that methods are not too lengthy or complex for the responding student.

Interviews and Focus Groups

For as long as people have held opinions, others have been asking them to give voice to their thoughts. Interviews and focus groups represent two methods of data collection in which the questioner seeks rich information from participants. There are a number of reasons for conducting interviews or focus groups. They may be used to better understand people or situations that interviewers know little about, to more definitively explain survey results, or to plan more in-depth assessments. Ultimately, collected responses may provide deeper levels of information and understanding (Bresciani, Zelna, & Anderson, 2004; Suskie, 2009).

Whereas interviews consist of one individual answering a question at a time, focus groups typically represent small numbers of people (usually alike in some way) fielding questions together (Suskie, 2009). In either case, the discussion generally follows one of three formats: structured, semi-structured, and unstructured (Schuh, 2009). Structured interviews are deliberate conversations in which the interviewer closely follows a script. This technique provides consistency in language but generally prevents the interviewer from asking follow-up questions of participants, thereby increasing the chance of missed opportunities to collect further data (Schuh, 2009).

As with structured interviews, semi-structured conversations provide the interviewer with an initial protocol or guide for the questioning. However, as the participant(s) respond, the interviewer has the freedom to explore additional topics as they arise or ask follow-up questions to gain deeper understanding (Schuh, 2009).

Unstructured interviews are free-form conversations in which interviewers are not tied to a script or guide. Questions may arise based on participants' answers or observations, and these interviews provide the greatest amount of freedom to interviewers (Schuh, 2009).

Regardless of the format selected, it is critical to conduct more than one interview or focus group. To not do so not only limits the information collected, but also increases the likelihood of a single person or group of people acting as "opinion drivers," thereby skewing the data (Suskie, 2009). That said, conducting multiple interviews or focus groups may still result in conversations with a number of difficult or challenging participants. Questioners can minimize or altogether avoid these challenges by first establishing rapport with the subject(s), then establishing a set of ground rules to guide the discussion (Bresciani, Zelna, & Anderson, 2004).

Ultimately, deciding whether to conduct individual interviews or focus groups depends on a number of factors. These factors may include the topic, time frame, size of population, assistance, budget, and ease of repeatability. Of course, one may opt to use both interviews and focus groups (Bresciani, Zelna, & Anderson, 2004).

Recently, the Student Leader Learning Outcomes (SLLO) project at Texas A&M University sought to determine what experiences influenced positional student leaders both personally and academically (SLLO, 2011). It was hoped that the information collected would shed light on how and what positional leaders might learn from their leadership experience. While the potential population was large (at the time, the university recognized more than 800 student organizations), the nature of the topic and the project goals dictated a conversational approach. Fortunately, the time frame for the project was not limiting, and assistance was readily available for interviews and data analysis. With the aforementioned criteria met, a number of SLLO volunteers from the Division of Student Affairs solidified a plan to interview students individually.

Once the decision is made to use focus groups and/or interviews, a proper protocol should be developed. As previously discussed, there are a number of potential formats to use. Whatever the format, consistency in delivery is important. At the start of each discussion, the questioner should have a prepared purpose statement and provide identical directions to the participant(s) (Suskie, 2009).

For the SLLO interviews, staff members were provided a series of instructions. Specifically, these outlined the nature of the study, informed participants what types of questions they would be asked, detailed how the information would be used, and assured each individual of confidentiality. Once this information was relayed, each participant was given a consent form to sign, which detailed the previously delivered information. Finally, each participant was given an opportunity to ask questions before the interview began.

Once participants are familiarized with the purpose and format of the discussion, the interviewer may begin posing questions. As interviews and focus groups are opportunities to collect information via in-depth participant responses, the most effective question types are generally those that are open-ended and require more participant dialogue than a simple yes or no (Suskie, 2009). Beyond this, Suskie recommends questions that are brief, singular (i.e., ask one question at a time), clearly understandable, and focused and do not ask for broad generalizations, attitudes, or opinions. Moreover, interviewers should avoid questions that participants may interpret as being "biased, loaded, leaning, or sensitive" (Suskie, 2004, p. 232).

The SLLO interviews were semi-structured conversations consisting of a series of core questions documented in the Student Leader Learning Project Interview Protocol (see Appendix B). In the course of each interview, staff members had opportunities to ask follow-up questions of participants. While they were not to veer off topic, interviewers were given some freedom to explore themes related to the purpose of the study if the occasion arose. Between questions, interviewers were provided with consistent transition phrases to shift the conversation from one subject to the next.

Another decision in any interview project is to determine the appropriate number of interviews or focus groups to host. Two factors may inform this decision, namely saturation and variation. Saturation results when participant responses become repetitive across a number of interviews or focus groups. Variation relates to the makeup of a given interview or focus group pool (Bresciani, Zelna, & Anderson, 2004). In other words, the individuals questioned should reflect the broader population being studied. Failing to collect responses from sufficiently diverse individuals may produce results that, while saturated, are inaccurate (Bresciani, Zelna, & Anderson, 2004). Although the SLLO group could have conducted interviews with more than a thousand positional student leaders, they opted to conduct approximately 40 interviews, a number large enough for appropriate variation and saturation.

Making sense of the data collected can be confusing and overwhelming. As interviews and focus groups produce varied responses, these formats rely on qualitative analysis to identify common themes (Suskie, 2009). There are a number of methods used to conduct qualitative analysis, and deciding which method to use may depend on the initial purpose of the study. If specific information is being sought, it may be appropriate to use predetermined rubrics. If, however, questioners are not bound to pre-identified results or if the interviews or focus groups result in unexpected responses, open coding may be a more effective method to group like data (Bresciani, Zelna, & Anderson, 2004). When coding interview responses, the SLLO research team opted for the latter method as there was a wide range of responses.

Interviews and focus groups can provide deep, interesting information, but remember that this technique also takes more time to implement and analyze. As with other assessment methods, you may want to pilot the questions with a couple of students so you know your questions are understandable and purposeful. Seek out resources on campus or from texts devoted to qualitative methods.

Portfolios

Portfolios represent incredible opportunities to gauge student learning and the overall effectiveness of a class or program. Portfolios exist in many forms—paper, electronic, or mixed media (Bresciani, Zelna, & Anderson, 2004). Although paper portfolios provide tangible examples of work, electronic portfolios offer many benefits, including ease of storage, increased variety in the types of usable artifacts, and simplicity of navigation through the use of menus and hyperlinks (Huba & Freed, 2000). Regardless of the format, most portfolios include content independently determined by each student, as well as student reflections (Huba & Freed, 2000). As each student's portfolio is unique, portfolios collectively provide diverse and personalized evidence of learning (Suskie, 2009). For reviewers, portfolios may also reveal a student's level of self-awareness and demonstrate not only what but *how* each student learns (Huba & Freed, 2000). In addition, portfolios may serve to identify achievement gaps when compared to learning or program outcomes (Suskie, 2009).

While portfolios can effectively measure individual student growth, one must first consider the purpose before opting to use this method of assessment (Huba & Freed, 2000). Effective portfolios are "woven into the curriculum and cocurriculum to capture ongoing student work" over a course or over the student's time in college (Banta, Griffin, Flateby, & Kahn, 2009, p. 8). Completed portfolios can be used to evaluate learning by including finished products to demonstrate what a typical student achieves in a given program (Huba & Freed, 2000). Moreover, portfolios can also reveal what changes might be made to a program or course. If the program has stated outcomes but evidence for achieving these outcomes is not present in the portfolio, administrators may be better equipped to make specific curriculum decisions to improve the experience (Bresciani, Zelna, & Anderson, 2004). Because of the time required to assemble and evaluate portfolios, this method of assessment is generally best suited for small numbers of participants in longer-term experiences (Huba & Freed, 2000; Suskie, 2009).

There are several issues to consider when determining whether or not to use portfolios. First, determine the goals for the assessment. According to Suskie (2009), portfolios may be best suited to reveal cognitive growth as opposed to fact recitation. Therefore, using this method of assessment to determine a student's ability to recall important historical dates may not be the most effective measure.

Second, identify the audience. The audience may simply consist of the individuals assembling their respective portfolios, but it may also include the staff members who developed the course or program, members of the department's leadership team, or even individuals in the local community. Understanding who will ultimately view the completed portfolios can help shape the content requirements.

Third, consider the selection process. Effective portfolios often provide evaluation criteria to students while allowing them the freedom to determine what evidence to include (Suskie, 2009). This process provides students the opportunity to self-reflect and decide what work best represents their successes. That said, portfolios are excellent tools to measure lengthy participant involvement, demonstrating growth with longitudinal evidence from each student's experience (Suskie, 2009). Therefore, program administrators may opt to ask for early drafts or project outlines in addition to the final products.

Fourth, provide an appropriate reflection process. Not only can the act of reflection increase a student's sense of self-awareness, but the reflection itself also demonstrates participant learning in a direct and measurable fashion (Huba & Freed, 2000; Suskie, 2009). Portfolio reflections can take a number of forms, from in-class discussions to written responses accompanying each portfolio artifact. In addition to asking each student to explain why he or she selected a particular artifact, administrators may wish to ask the students what they learned from each project, how these lessons could be applied to other realms of their lives, or what they would have done differently if starting the project again from scratch. Portfolios without reflections are not tools for assessment; they are simply collections of work (Huba & Freed, 2000).

Fifth, develop an evaluation process. This may consist of a scoring rubric, a summary, or student reflections (Bresciani, Zelna, & Anderson, 2004). Ultimately, an effective portfolio should assemble "in one place evidence of many different kinds of learning and skills. It encourages students, faculty, and staff to examine student learning holistically—seeing how learning comes together—rather than through compartmentalized skills and knowledge" (Suskie, 2009, p. 204).

Finally, determine what happens with portfolios as they are completed. In many cases, students may keep their assembled portfolios and continue adding to them for future use with job interviews or graduate school. In some cases, however, program administrators may opt to keep the final portfolios as a reference or to showcase the work to future students. Knowing what will become of the portfolios at the outset allows administrators to answer questions throughout the process and better guide students in the artifact selection process.

Though time-consuming for all parties, portfolios can provide tremendous benefits to both students and staff (Huba & Freed, 2000). For students, portfolios generate opportunities to consider their individual learning styles and better understand how they make meaning from experience. Completed portfolios demonstrating the evolution of a project from start to finish can help students, their advisors, and even future employers better understand the thought process of the individual. Portfolios also promote creative expression in demonstrating how students learn, allowing them to place emphasis on what was most influential throughout their developmental process (Slater, 1997). The implementation of fine arts activities such as photography and creative writing are being used more regularly as media for learning assessment (Slater, 1994; Collins, 1992, 1993).

Portfolio reflection can also draw on curricular and cocurricular experience, linking the two in ways traditional exams may not. Simply asking students to connect the lessons learned from the creation of the portfolio to classes, jobs, or relationships with others encourages them to link previously disparate experiences. Suddenly, one's experience in a student organization can begin to inform work in future class projects and vice versa. Written communication, public speaking, and working in teams are clear examples of the overlap of the curricular and cocurricular environments.

Students completing portfolios often "become more aware of and invested in their own learning" (Huba & Freed, 2000, p. 263). When faced with the realization of all they have accomplished—often in a format they largely dictated themselves—students may begin to embrace learning as a self-driven process (as opposed to one that is staff or teacher driven).

For staff, the portfolio experience may afford opportunities to develop more personal relationships with individual students. Students generally have great control of the content of their portfolios, presenting staff members with excellent opportunities to learn about each individual student. Questioning why one artifact was included over another or simply understanding why and how each artifact was important to each individual student can provide great insight.

As the portfolio generally calls for student reflections, staff may also increase their awareness of each student's unique "strengths, weaknesses, and needs," (Huba & Freed, 2000, p. 260). This information can prove helpful to staff or faculty in other realms of advising or teaching and possibly can increase the overall effectiveness of the program or class.

Banta, Griffin, Flateby, and Kahn (2009) summarized some of the advantages and disadvantages of using electronic portfolios. On the plus side, portfolios represent ongoing class assignments and cocurricular work; artifacts represent long-term, cognitively complex activities; students are engaged in the learning process and their own development; and portfolios can be assessed using rubrics, which can yield a reasonably reliable score. On the minus side, electronic portfolios are relatively new on campuses, so longitudinal data are not available; because the technology is fairly new, few software products meet all of the campus needs; and "increased contextual validity, an important strength of portfolios, often comes at the expense of reliability" (p. 11).

Perhaps most important for both parties, portfolios developed over a period of time provide staff and students ways to "engage in substantive discussions . . . that promote learning," (Huba & Freed, 2000, p. 260). Questioning why and how a particular piece of evidence fits in the portfolio, asking what was learned, and discussing ways in which the program or class could be improved are all excellent avenues for staff and students alike to learn from one another. Although these conversations could happen with other measures of student learning, the process of portfolio assembly and the continual opportunities for reflection make this an excellent tool for thorough, informed discussions.

Pre- and Post-tests

Using pre- and post-tests, or value-added tools, can demonstrate growth over a period of time (Suskie, 2009). Designed to collect the same information each time they are administered, value-added assessments allow staff the opportunity to witness participant growth (Suskie, 2009). These types of tools may include quantitative questions or the use of identical prompts at varied points throughout an experience.

For example, in an attempt to measure the effectiveness of programs and events, the Leadership and Service Center (LSC) in the Department of Student Activities at Texas A&M University developed a series of 11 centerwide outcomes. Each outcome was associated with a series of statements to be included on program pre- and post-assessments. Program participants indicated their level of agreement with each statement (e.g., "I believe others see me as a leader"), thereby providing staff in the center with an indicator of the success of the program related to each outcome. As each statement used a Likert scale to indicate each student's level of agreement, the results were easily quantifiable.

The LSC also made use of several open-ended questions on assessments. Asking students to respond to the question "How might you apply information you learned today to other areas of your life?" provided open opportunities for students to reflect on what they learned and how that knowledge, skill, or ability could be put to use in other arenas. This information could then be used to further inform (or call into question) data provided by the previously mentioned outcome statements.

At the conclusion of the academic year, the LSC was able to compare programs with like outcomes because participants had responded to the same statements on each evaluation. When joined with other factors such as program attendance, cost, and qualitative statements, the LSC was able to better understand a program's effectiveness.

Though once a more common form of assessment, these types of measures have more recently become less widely used for a number of reasons (Suskie, 2009). Students who are aware of the use of pre- and post-assessments may be less motivated to try on the pre-assessment. A simplistic example may occur each semester in physical education courses, where students might be asked to run a timed mile on the first day of class and again on the last. Thinking their grade is dependent on demonstrating great improvement in their individual times, students may choose to run more slowly than they are capable on the first run. When applied to student learning, individuals could understate their knowledge, skills, or abilities if they associate growth in capability with a positive outcome.

Another possibility is that students may overestimate their knowledge, skills, or abilities on the pre-test. In many cases, the pre-test is the first time a group of students are asked to reflect on a specific set of questions. If they are not motivated to consider their experience or if they have never done so in comparison to others, their initial confidence may be overstated. Sometimes students don't know what they do not know.

Another concern arises when scoring qualitative work. Individual scorers may use different criteria, leading to inconsistent results even if a rubric is used. While this effect can be limited by having one individual read and score all pre- and post-writings (perhaps using a rubric), there are still opportunities for variation dependent on the scorer's mood, energy, or level of distraction. Inter-rater reliability must be addressed for consistency.

Finally, regardless of the type of assessment, it is difficult to assess whether or not any growth in learning was caused by a specific program or course. For example, students in a social justice class may demonstrate growth between the pre- and post-tests in their awareness of issues facing the local community. However, if an event occurs in the community during the semester (perhaps with campus and local news coverage), students in the social justice class may have gained their increased awareness from these outlets as opposed to the course. While the assessment may ask students to consider questions only in light of the course or program material, there is no guarantee they will do so.

In brief, pre- and post-tests can be simple and efficient ways to quantify and report findings. However, with their reliance on student self-reporting, these types of assessments are vulnerable to manipulation and might be most effective when used in conjunction with other assessment methods.

Learning Contracts

As one might assume, learning contracts are agreements between parties specifying what knowledge or skill is to be learned, how the knowledge or skill will be learned, and how each party will know that the knowledge or skill has been learned (Codde, 2006). These agreements generally specify a time frame for completion, be it one month, one semester, or one academic year. Ultimately, learning contracts empower students to become active participants in their own learning, making them responsible not only for learning the specified knowledge or skill contained in the contract, but also for mastering the tools necessary to become self-directed learners in the future (Codde, 2006).

Though potentially time consuming to use, learning contracts present numerous benefits to students. First, as they are specific to individuals, learning contracts allow staff to meet the diverse learning needs and styles of each student (Codde, 2006). For example, one program may ask participants to expand their understanding of leadership. While the overall outcome is the same, one student may wish to do so by taking a class, another by interviewing subjects, and still another by becoming a positional leader in a student organization. In the end, each individual will have had opportunities to achieve the outcome, but the paths taken to do so will look different for each of them.

Second, as with portfolios, students play an important role in determining the content of the contract and become "active participants in the creation of knowledge rather than passive recipients" (Codde, 2006, p. 1). They can involve themselves in decisions about the list of achievement targets, their varied strategies for reaching each target, and how they will ultimately measure their effectiveness.

Finally, students using learning contracts have been shown to maintain increased motivation in the accomplishment of the contract goals (Lewis, 2004). At their best, learning contracts developed with students can motivate them to take charge of their learning and begin setting and achieving self-generated goals.

The specific language of learning contracts may vary from use to use; however, they should contain several key components. Generally, these include a specified objective, a detailed plan to accomplish the objective, a target date for completion, what evidence will be presented to demonstrate completion of the objective, and what measure will be used to evaluate the evidence (Codde, 2006).

While it may be tempting to write learning contracts like a legal document, remember they represent learning agreements between a student and an advisor, employer, or faculty member. The language is far less important than the fact that the document should help the students clearly identify what they want to learn, how they will learn it, and how they (and the staff member) will know they have reached their goal. For that reason, success depends on active participation from each party. Students may be intimidated by formality (or even the word "contract"), so the language can vary as long as the parties agree on the meaning.

As with many of the methods discussed in this chapter, learning contracts can represent a significant time investment for everyone. However, the benefits of student-directed, self-motivated learning can far outweigh the cost should this method be a viable option.

Conclusion

In the final stages of assessment, it is imperative to revisit a few of the questions that shaped our student development goals, such as what do we want students to learn, what methods were used to facilitate that process, and how was their progress measured? Advisors should also be concerned about whether or not there is a direct correlation between student learning and the program objectives. One last method that may assist in ensuring that all goals are met is the calculated use of documented observations.

Observations by advisors and supervisors are an effective way to evaluate the overall assessment process and many times can be all-encompassing of other methods. They are typically organized into two parts: (1) identifying student strengths and accomplishments in addition to their inefficiencies or areas for growth and (2) making recommendations for improved development based on learning outcome objectives (Cartwright, Weiner & Streamer-Veneruso, 2009). However, observation without the proper documentation that learning took place is anecdotal at best. It is the documentation *and* the observation by the student affairs professional that is needed to assist student leaders as they learn, develop, and grow while achieving the outcomes established by our institutions.

As stated in the introduction, the primary goal of this chapter is to explore ways to effectively measure learning outcomes. Therefore, the observation process offers a variety of methods for demonstrating learning significance and skill enhancement through documentation. Many of these associated tools are reflective and often assume the use of journals, photography, video and audio recordings, checklists, and portfolios (Suskie, 2009; Huba & Freed, 2000; Slater, n.d.). Interestingly enough, documentation through observation may even allow for creative expression as students may be inspired to articulate their progress through constructing photo collages, scrapbooks, or websites.

Advisors should also consider taking anecdotal notes as a form of observation. Simply writing down comments on sticky notes or index cards is an easy and efficient way to monitor student progress and enhanced performance. These notes can be transcribed and compiled into a notebook or binder for later review (Department of Education, n.d.) and reflection. Collecting notes for each student on a daily basis may turn out to be too arduous. However, using spontaneity in conjunction with intentionality in reporting can ensure that students are fulfilling the gamut of their learning potential (Department of Education, n.d.). For student organization advisors who meet with their top student leader on a regular basis, keeping a journal could be integrated into that natural process.

Advisors should be aware that, when making observations, consistency in linking experiential activities directly to the learning outcomes is just as vital to their own synthesis process as it is for their students (Department of Education, n.d.). Established outcomes should be tailored to each student's respective abilities and aptitude for learning within the culture of the organization. Hence, the advisor is governed by authenticity and accountability when supporting the progress of each student. Collecting a series of work samples also helps to keep abreast of student accomplishments and deficiencies.

Dated works organized chronologically can denote progress in abilities and skills in a similar fashion to portfolios (Department of Education, n.d.).

In closing the loop with assessment, it may be beneficial to create a detailed checklist to make certain that all aspects of the process have been completed. Checklist items could include the name of the participant group, learning outcome objectives, assessment tools or methods used, duration of the assessment, the scope of implementation, the duration of observations, results of the assessment, and commonly used terms or definitions, in addition to any recommendations or concerns. Typically, best practices are then identified on one end, and an action plan for improvement is devised on the other (Cartwright, Weiner, & Streamer-Veneruso, 2009).

The final phase of assessment entails pulling together all of the lessons learned by students and being able to articulate specifically how they have grown throughout their respective journeys. This rule does not apply only to them; it also pertains to advisors or assessment administrators. Just as designing clear and measurable learning outcomes is an integral part of the assessment process, so too is facilitating meaningful interactions with students. We must always keep in mind that the learning experiences and feedback that occur through interpersonal exchange and authentic mentoring have far more impact than any assessment strategy. Knowing this, it is clear that no method can ever be effective without the use of that most invaluable tool.

Questions for Reflection

1. What assessment methods appeal to you? Why?
2. What resources do you need in order to document student learning in the cocurricular environment?
3. What challenges do you foresee in assessing student learning?

References

Allen, D., & Tanner, K. (2006). Rubrics: Tools for making learning goals and evaluation criteria explicit for both teachers and learners. *CBE–Life Sciences Education, 5,* 197–203.

Ash, S. L., Clayton, P. H., & Atkinson, M. P. (2005). Integrating reflection and assessment to capture and improve student learning. *Michigan Journal of Community Service Learning, 11*(2), 49–60.

Banta, T. W., Griffin, M., Flateby, T. L., & Kahn, S. (2009, December). *Three promising alternatives for assessing college students' knowledge and skills.* (NILOA Occasional Paper No. 2). Urbana, IL: University of Illinois and Indiana University, National Institute of Learning Outcomes Assessment.

Baxter Magolda, M. B., & King, P. M. (2008). Toward reflective conversations: An advising approach that promotes self-authorship. *Peer Review, 10*(1), 8–11.

Beam, M. (2005, June). *Survey design and process.* Retrieved from http://www.mtsac. edu/administration/research/pdf/tips/SurveyDesignandProcess.pdf

Bresciani, M. J., Zelna, C. L., & Anderson, J. A. (2004). *Assessing student learning and development: A handbook for practitioners.* Washington, DC: National Association of Student Personnel Administrators.

Cartwright, R., Weiner, K., & Streamer-Veneruso, S. (2009). *Student learning outcomes assessment handbook.* Retrieved from http://www.montgomerycollege.edu/ Departments/outcomes/documents/sloa_handbook.pdf

Codde, J. R. (2006). *Using learning contracts in the college classroom.* Retrieved from https://www.msu.edu/user/coddejos/contract.htm

Collins, A. (1992). Portfolios for science education: Issues in purpose, structure, and authenticity. *Science Education, 76*(4), 451–463.

Collins, A. (1993). Performance-based assessment of biology teachers. *Journal of College Science Teaching, 30*(9), 1103–1120.

Department of Education, Newfoundland Labrador, Canada. (n.d.). *Assessment techniques and tools for documentation.* Retrieved from https://dsacms.tamu.edu/ sites/sllo.tamu.edu/files/LearningContractGuidelines.pdf

Huba, M. E., & Freed, J. E. (2000). *Learner-centered assessment on college campuses: Shifting the focus from teaching to learning.* Needham Heights, MA: Allyn & Bacon.

Lewis, J. J. (2004). The independent learning contract system: Motivating students enrolled in college reading courses. *Reading Improvement, 41*(3), 188–194.

Luft, J.A. (1999). Rubrics: design and use in science teacher education. *Journal of Science Teacher Education, 10*(2), 107–121.

Muirhead, B. (2002). Relevant assessment strategies for online colleges and universities. *USDLA Journal.* Retrieved from http://www.usdla.org/html/journal/FEB02_Issue/article04.html

Rhodes, T. (Ed.). (2010). *Assessing outcomes and improving achievement: Tips and tools for using rubrics.* Washington, DC: Association of American Colleges and Universities.

Schuh, J. H. (2009). *Assessment methods for student affairs.* San Francisco: Jossey-Bass.

Slater, T. F. (1994). Portfolio assessment strategies for introductory physics. *The Physics Teacher, 32*(6), 415–417.

Slater, T. F. (1997). The effectiveness of portfolio assessments in science. *Journal of College Science Teaching, 26*(5), 315–318.

Slater, T. F. (n.d). *Portfolio assessment.* Retrieved from http://www.flaguide.org/extra/download/cat/portfolios/portfolios.rtf

Stevens, D. D., & Levi, A. J. (2005). *Introduction to rubrics: An assessment tool to save grading time, convey effective feedback and promote student learning.* Sterling, VA: Stylus Publishing.

Student Leader Learning Outcomes (SLLO). (2011a). [Interview protocol]. Unpublished raw data.

Student Leader Learning Outcomes (SLLO). (2011b). [Student leader interviews]. Unpublished raw data.

Suskie, L. (2004). *Assessing student learning: A common sense guide.* Bolton, MA: Anker Publishing Company.

Suskie, L. (2009). *Assessing student learning: A common sense approach* (2nd ed.). San Francisco, CA: Jossey-Bass.

Tuckman, B. W., & Jensen, M. C. (1977). Stages of small group development revisited. *Group and Organizational Studies, 2*(4), 419–426

TEAMS AND GROUPS RUBRIC

Name of Student:		Date Completed:			
TEAMS AND GROUPS OUTCOMES	**NOVICE**	**TRANSITION**	**INTERMEDIATE**	**TRANSITION**	**ADVANCED**
	Awareness or Base-level Knowledge	From Novice to Intermediate	Apply the Concept Somewhat	From Intermediate to Advanced	Intentional and Effective Application
Forming	Does not recognize the need for assistance and advisor initiates conversation regarding safe place, orientation, and interpersonal barriers.		Recognizes need for assistance and initiates conversation with advisor to seek guidance and resources regarding safe place, orientation, and interpersonal barriers.		Independently creates a safe place and comfortable atmosphere with little to no advising; identifies resources to orient group to task or function and breaks down interpersonal barriers.
Storming	Does not recognize the need for assistance and advisor initiates conversation regarding constructive and appropriate conflict, group task and purpose, and safe space.		Recognizes need for assistance and initiates conversation with advisor to seek guidance and resources regarding constructive and appropriate conflict, group task and purpose, and safe space.		Independently encourages and facilitates constructive and appropriate conflict; reminds group of task and purpose of group; maintains safe space; ensures all can speak.

Norming	Does not recognize the need for assistance and advisor initiates conversation regarding trust and cohesion, communication, feedback, and interdependence.		Recognizes need for assistance and initiates conversation with advisor to seek guidance and resources regarding trust and cohesion, communication, feedback, and interdependence.		Independently moves group from conflict to trust and cohesion; communication issues are resolved; feedback is solicited and given freely; group comes together around task and interdependence develops.
Performing	Does not recognize the need for assistance and advisor initiates conversation regarding being less directive and more supportive, serving as a resource, and delegating.		Recognizes need for assistance and initiates conversation with advisor to seek guidance and resources regarding being less directive and more supportive, serving as a resource, and delegating.		Independently recognizes the need to step back and be less directive and more supportive and encouraging; serves as a resource for the group; delegates; members are confident in their ability to complete tasks.
Adjourning	Does not recognize the need for assistance and advisor initiates conversation regarding evaluation of group's work, facilitating reflection, recognizing and celebrating accomplishments, and beginning closure through disengagement		Recognizes need for assistance and initiates conversation with advisor to seek guidance and resources regarding evaluation of group's work, facilitating reflection, recognizing and celebrating accomplishments, and beginning closure through disengagement.		Independently initiates evaluation of groups' work; facilitates reflection; recognizes and celebrates accomplishments; begins bringing closure to work through disengagement process; asks questions such as "Should group continue?"

COMMENTS:

STUDENT LEADER LEARNING OUTCOMES PROJECT INTERVIEW PROTOCOL

Opening statement in your own words:

- I will be asking you questions about your leadership experiences and how they have impacted you both academically and personally
- The information gathered will help the Student Leadership Learning Outcomes project understand how and what students learn in their leadership experiences
- All the information you provide will be completely confidential and will not be ascribed to you personally
- It is our hope that the information we collect during this project will help advisors and peer educators be more purposeful and supportive of student learning in their student organization or work experiences

I have a consent form that explains what I have just told you and allows us to record this interview to assure that we have an accurate record of what you share with us. (Have the interviewee sign and date the form s/he keeps one and you keep the other.)

Begin the recording by stating your name, the date, and the first name of the person you are interviewing.

Interview questions to be asked exactly as they appear here.

1. Tell me about the leadership experiences you have had since starting your journey through Aggieland.
   - We are looking for a general overview here—almost a listing of experiences— not an in depth discussion of each experience

Transition: My first question is about the relationship between your classroom and student leadership experiences.

2. What have you learned in your leadership experiences that has contributed to your academics?
    -   Rephrased: Have you used the learning from your leadership experiences in your classes?
    -   If yes, can you give me a specific example?

3. Another way to look at your leadership experiences is to ask the last question in reverse. What have you learned in your classes that you have been able to apply to your leadership experiences?
    -   Can you give me a specific example?

    Transition: The next questions ask you to reflect on your leadership strengths and how you came to develop them.

4. What are your strongest leadership strengths or skills?
    -   It is fine if the student identifies strengths rather than skills

5. What do you do now in your leadership role that you didn't do in your first leadership role?
    -   How did you accomplish that change or improvement?
    -   What was the evidence you used that confirmed you had changed or improved?

6. How were you challenged to grow or stretch yourself?
    -   Another way to frame this question or to continue the interviewee's discussion: What risks were you willing to take? (Not risk in a risk management sense, but risk that took you beyond your current comfort zone with your capabilities and experience.)

7. Give me an example of your biggest achievement as a leader of your current (or just past) student organization?

    Transition: The next question is directed at understanding the bigger picture of the impact of your leadership experiences on you personally.

8. Do you think your leadership experiences have affected your personal values and beliefs?
    *   If yes, can you give me an example?
    *   If no, can you elaborate on why those values and beliefs have not been affected.
        o   Were they ever challenged?

    Transition: Before we close our interview, I want you to have a chance to tell me anything I may have missed.

9. Is there anything you would like to share about your leadership experiences that we have not discussed?
    *   If you don't have time for this question, it is okay.

Thank you very much for your time today. If you would like to know the outcome of this interviewing project, just give me your contact information if the email we have for you will be changing.

Note. Copyright © 2011 by Student Life Studies, Texas A&M University. Reproduced with permission.

CHAPTER 5

STUDENT ORGANIZATION ADVISORS AND STUDENT EMPLOYEE SUPERVISORS

Who is Responsible for the Process?

Katy King

"Being given the opportunity to be part of not only my student learning but in the growth and development of the people I was leading would not have been possible without the encouragement, direction, and example set by my advisor."
–Jessica Licarione, former student, Texas A&M University

Like many student affairs professionals, I had no idea that "this" is what I was going to be doing with my life. I began college as an accounting major, eventually graduating with a marketing degree but driven to live a life in student affairs. However, even after two years submerged in student development theory and eagerly awaiting my first job in the profession, I was focused on the event planning, advising, and mentoring aspects of the job. The "student learning" piece was covered by my academic partners, right? Why would my *supervisor* ever need to know what I was doing to supplement and encourage student learning? I was helping to organize fundraisers, service-learning projects, and leadership retreats. My assumption was that surely this was enough. I was surprised to learn how much more my job in student affairs would entail, especially when it came to student learning.

Many times, our jobs seem to require much more than what is stated in the position descriptions. We soon discover that "other duties as assigned" can entail a lot of additional tasks, including responsibility for creating opportunities for student learning in campus activities. At first glance, many advisors/supervisors assume the concept of documenting learning is outside the scope of their role; the job is centered on managing time, projects, budgets, and risk, among other things. However, in the current economic climate, in which many of us are facing budget cuts, hiring freezes, and elimination of positions, our success in educating student leaders can reinforce to the campus community and other constituents the need for student affairs staff.

Student learning in campus activities is important and can link student affairs to academic partners, creating validity in our work. Throughout the process of creating the Student Leader Learning Outcomes (SLLO) project at Texas A&M University, our team discovered that documenting learning did not add any unnecessary work to our jobs; rather, the process added meaning and depth. Our work became different, and that difference benefited our students. Throughout this chapter, you will discover how to integrate into your daily practice a focus on student learning and understand what to look for in individual students as well as entire organizations.

Commit to Learning

Student affairs has been analyzing its commitment to learning for years. Through documents such as *Learning Reconsidered* (Keeling, 2004) and *Learning Reconsidered 2* (Keeling, 2006), we know that a focused effort on student learning is an essential and core component of the student experience. These two publications and others created excitement across college campuses. They asked student affairs professionals to answer the important question, "How do we become more involved in student learning?" Whitt (2006) offered 10 lessons to student affairs professionals who are, or want to be, engaged in the student learning process. Her conclusions were based on a review of 24 colleges and universities that participated in Project DEEP (Documenting Effective Educational Practice) through the National Survey of Student Engagement. These 10 conclusions recognized involvement needed across the institution:

- **Focus on student learning. Period.** Student affairs staff, mission, programs, etc. support the educational mission of the institution. Students can articulate their learning in relation to the institution outcomes.
- **Create and sustain partnerships for learning.** Academic affairs, student affairs, and students create a collaborative learning environment that values education.
- **Hold all students to high expectations for engagement and learning, in and out of the classroom, on and off campus.** Students must take advantage of all kinds of experiences and resources to realize the full impact of involvement.
- **Implement a comprehensive set of safety nets and early warning systems.** Student affairs staff have great potential to know students on a personal basis and steer them in the direction of services that can enhance success.
- **Teach new students what it takes to succeed.** Programs are provided for new students that can be integrated into the curriculum and address transition issues.
- **Recognize, affirm, and celebrate the educational value of diversity.** Experiences are infused into all areas of learning and provide an opportunity for self-reflection.
- **Invest in programs and people that demonstrate contributions to student learning and success.** Institutions invest resources (money, time, space, and staff) to promote effective learning practices.
- **Use data to inform decisions.** Institutions systematically collect information as well as personal experiences to inform practice and planning.
- **Create spaces for learning.** Use new construction projects to create facilities that enhance teaching and influence the learning environment. These spaces should be accessible to students and others including hours of operation and the provision of appropriate resources.
- **Make every residence hall a learning community.** Residence hall staff offer programs, services, and learning communities that support the educational mission. (pp. 3–8)

The process of integrating learning into the cocurricular environment should be shared with your student leaders—it *requires* buy-in from your chief members, as well as advocacy from supervisors for the advisor/supervisor to guide organizations in this way. Without the student voice, this process is lost. Communicating the benefits of this approach to leadership development is also a key element. Students, like staff, want to understand the value of a concept before deciding whether to take the first step. Finally, as a professional, your time is valuable. In establishing a working relationship with your organization(s), students, and supervisor, you need to define the amount of time and energy that you are able to commit to your duties.

The key to creating buy-in from students is to make the assignments or integration tools useful, meaningful, and relevant to the student users. Also, understand that buy-in will not always be immediate. Students, like anyone else, need time to adjust to change, and the concept of integrating learning into a leadership experience includes a lot of adjustment. Even the most advanced student leaders may need time to process this concept. Komives, Lucas, and McMahon (2007) stated, "[C]hange is very difficult, challenging work that usually causes leaders to be filled with self-doubt.... [S]tudents [may] come up with many reasons to not get involved in change efforts" (p. 353).

By sharing the responsibility for student learning, staff and students together can create a relationship that will produce outcomes that are beneficial to all. A crucial part in creating this relationship is evaluating your role and duties as an advisor/supervisor. In addition, you must assess with your students the role they want you to play in the organizational setting.

Advising 101

As a student organization advisor or student employee supervisor, you will be called on to serve in a variety of roles that are unique to a particular student organization or employee group. But when focusing advising efforts on student learning, the same concepts apply. In preparing for your advising experience, you must first determine the role you will play in the organization. Dunkel and Schuh (1998) identified five roles that an advisor can play while working with students and organizations:

1. **Mentor:** Models behaviors and values that a younger person admires and respects.
2. **Supervisor:** Utilizes position to empower leadership and follows a series of practices that may include team building, planning, communication, recognition, self-assessment, and evaluation.
3. **Teacher:** Encourages students to invest time inside the classroom as academic success leads to cocurricular involvement.
4. **Leader:** Educates students in identifying the power they possess in leading others.
5. **Follower:** Assists student leaders in identifying the expectations of their followers/membership. (p. 45)

When leading a group through uncommon ground, it's important to know which role you should assume. Dunkel and Schuh (1998) continued by stating that advisors often rely on comfort level when selecting their respective role. However, new concepts, ideas, and ways of doing things can often make the entire group feel uncomfortable.

Another concept to consider when exploring your role as advisor and supervisor is that of self-authorship. Baxter Magolda and King (2008) examined this role extensively. (See Chapters 2, 4, and 7 for more information on self-authorship.) Although the research was originally geared toward academic advisors, it can be easily adapted to student organization advisors and student employee supervisors. The advisor/supervisor/educator should initiate meaningful conversations and listen, but "the key element is encouraging students to make sense of their experience, rather than the educator making sense of it for them" (p. 9). Baxter Magolda and King proposed four general phases that could represent a single meeting, the academic year, or a particular leadership experience.

1. **Getting acquainted and building rapport.** Ask students about themselves, their expectations, and their experiences so far. Get students to talk deeply about their experiences and what they learned from them.

2. **Encouraging reflection about important experiences.** Have students fully explain significant, best, and/or worst experiences. Encourage students to examine the experiences from various angles (moving from what happened to why it was meaningful). Prompts could include questions about challenges, support systems, decision making, different perspectives, stressors, and joys.

3. **Encouraging interpretation of these reflections.** Challenge students to look at the big picture of their experiences and the impact on their identity, values, relationships, maturity, and future.

4. **Concluding thoughts.** Express appreciation for the student sharing their stories and reflections, encourage them to continue that process, and invite them to share future insights with you. (pp. 8–9)

The American College Personnel Association (ACPA) and the National Association of Student Personnel Administrators (NASPA) (2010) identified basic, intermediate, and advanced competencies ranging from active listening skills and establishing rapport with students to perceiving unspoken dynamics in a group and providing necessary staff training to enhance advising skills. Appendix C shows a tool based on the basic advising competencies that were identified. (Note that although this tool was created with student organization advisors in mind, many of the aspects of the chart also apply to student employee supervisors.) You and the student leaders you advise can complete this survey either before or during your regular meeting time. Space has been provided on the form to add institution-specific expectations or other important information. The key is to reach agreement about your role in the organization, an agreement that matches the student organization, the organization culture, your advising style, and the institution requirements. See Appendix D for other activities that help identify advisor and supervisor expectations.

It is the responsibility of the advisor/supervisor to lead with confidence and to create a foundation for the organization to stand on. Whether you use a specific model to identify your role, use self-authorship techniques, or develop your skills based on competencies such as those established by ACPA and NASPA, you have the ability to include how your group(s) embrace student learning.

Integrating Learning

Komives, Lucas, and McMahon (2007) stated, "The whole group of participants . . . needs to make sure the environment is open to learning. . . . Any behaviors or circumstances that block learning in organizations are likely to block empowerment and inclusion as well" (p. 26). In other words, when we as professionals evaluate our role, one of the most important contributions we can make to any campus is to create an inclusive environment. Can this really be accomplished by simply flipping a switch and integrating learning into the roles of our leaders? What other impact can our being intentional about student learning have on our students?

When integrating learning into your group, you need to understand the importance of meeting the individual and group where they are, in terms of their readiness. It is important to integrate student learning slowly and intentionally as this process is most successful when done gradually and with a student-user base that is as eager to participate in this process as you are to apply it. The goal is for student leaders to not only learn from their leadership experience(s), but also to articulate that learning in a way that can be easily comprehended by anyone, from their peers to their future CEO. Students should also be able to apply the skills they developed to multiple settings. The advisor plays a key role in this process by challenging students to synthesize and evaluate experiences in multiple settings.

Climate Check

Chapter 4 identified several tools that advisors and supervisors may use in documenting learning in campus activities. However, before selecting a tool, one should examine the culture and readiness of the organization. Just as advisors and supervisors differ in their approach to leadership development, student organizations differ in their level of development. The advisor/supervisor is responsible for recognizing the development level of their organization and matching their skills and approach accordingly. Several models can be referenced when determining the organizational culture. Two models are shown here as examples that will be expanded upon later in the chapter:

1. **The Situational Advising Model** (Allen, 1981) identifies four stages of student organizations and recommends advising styles accordingly: infancy, adolescence, young adulthood and maturity.
2. **The Model of Group Development** (Tuckman & Jensen, 1977) categorizes student organizations into stages of forming, storming, norming, performing, and adjourning.

Both of these models are used frequently in student affairs; however, evaluating the climate of an organization may also be as simple as listening to group discussions. Ask yourself: Are group discussions in the student organization led by one individual, or is everyone able to contribute? Do meetings revolve around the mission of the organization, or do meetings involve tangents on a variety of topics not associated with the organization? Are student leaders engaged or distant? Do officers promote a healthy academic career? Examine the status of the organization's social media sites and usage: Is the webpage current? Is Facebook, Twitter, and other media used appropriately? These questions may help determine the health of the organization and whether the first step in advising should be focused on creating a strong foundation.

Using the tools and concepts above, you can easily identify the current state of the organization's climate and intentionally assist the organization as the leaders begin their journey of integrating learning into their practice. Once you believe that the organization is ready to integrate student learning into its program, the next step is to identify which tool(s) or method(s) to use in this process.

Stocking your tool kit

Chapter 4 identified a plethora of tools that can be used in the student learning process. Baida (2009) recommended using the Situational Advising Model (Allen, 1981) when selecting a rubric to use with your student organization. With small adaptation, this guide can assist you in deciding on other tools beyond rubrics to use when documenting student learning in an organization. Advisors are in a unique position to balance student development, the organization's purpose, and their own style in working with a group of students. Advisors meet students where they are but also challenge them to take reasonable risks for growth.

Allen's (1981) model is an easy-to-use guide, pointing practitioners in the right direction regardless of the student organization with which they are working. Allen identified four stages of an organization:

1. **Infancy:** Students demonstrate low levels of commitment to the organization, programming skills, and responsibility for their actions.
2. **Adolescence:** Students demonstrate increasing programming skills, interest, commitment, and responsibility.
3. **Young Adulthood:** Students demonstrate competency in programming and a continued increase in commitment, plus a willingness to take responsibility for their own actions.
4. **Maturity:** Students demonstrate a high degree of competence in programming and group skills, a strong commitment to the group, and a willingness to take responsibility for their own and their group's actions. (p. 35)

Effective advisors and supervisors will then match their own advising style to the developmental level of the student organization. The following four advising styles are from Allen (1981) and based on the stage of the organization:

- **Director:** Has a high concern for the end result but is not very concerned about the process. This matches with students in the Infancy stage.
- **Teacher/Director:** Exhibits a high concern for both product and process. Correlates with students in the Adolescence stage.
- **Advisor/Teacher:** Concern for product is low because students handle this when in the Young Adulthood stage; high concern for process. Correlates with students in the Young Adulthood stage.
- **Consultant:** Product concern and process concern both low because students assume responsibility in both areas. Students at this point are in the Maturity stage.

The process of moving from one stage of development to another is gradual as the organization moves toward maturity. To better assist the group to develop, the advisor/supervisor must use more than one method of integrating learning. In a mature organization, student leaders may take on the role of developing their peers, with the advisor in the background. In employment situations, students may supervise other students, a function that requires a level of confidence and knowledge. Table 1 depicts some of the various tools spotlighted in Chapter 4 for documenting student learning aligned with Allen's (1981) four stages of an organization.

Table 1

Selecting Appropriate Learning Tools for Student Organizations

Stage	Tools
Infancy	• One-minute paper • Leadership moments • Learning-centered questions
Adolescence	• Rubrics • Exit interviews
Young Adulthood	• Learning contracts • Rubrics with subcommittees • Pre- and post-tests
Maturity	• Learning contracts • Rubrics with subcommittees • Pre- and post-tests • Student-guided feedback sessions

The tools in Table 1 above can be defined as follows (for more information, see Chapter 4):

- **One-minute paper:** Short reflection activity where students are given a question to reflect upon. For example, "What is the biggest lesson you learned working on this project?"
- **Leadership moments:** Short exercise that can be lead by anyone at the beginning of a meeting to spark conversation or introspection. These are particularly helpful if outcomes based, but can be as simple as discussing a famous quote on leadership.
- **Learning-centered questions:** Asking questions at the beginning of each meeting based on what students have learned as opposed to general information. For example, ask a student, "What did you study in class today?" instead of asking, "What did you do this weekend?"
- **Rubrics:** A specific set of criteria for one area of a topic, used to assess skill level.
- **Exit interviews:** Focus on self-evaluation as it relates to learning in the cocurricular environment.

- **Learning contracts:** Individual plan for achieving specific goals and learning objectives during a student's leadership experience.
- **Pre- and Post-tests:** Surveys that are distributed to several organization members evaluating competencies based on outcomes set by student leadership. For best results, it is recommended to distribute mid-year with the final survey given at year's end.
- **Student-guided feedback sessions:** Peer-to-peer sessions where student leader provides feedback to student follower regarding specific skill level, competency, and areas of improvement. This tool can be partnered with rubrics to guide conversation.

To expand on Tuckman and Jensen (1977), in the Forming stage, group members determine pace, going through testing and an orientation process before entering the Storming stage, where conflict often ensues as members resist cohesion and conflict arises. In the Norming stage, cohesiveness develops among group members as they start to accept rules of behavior, and people establish how to work together. In the Performing stage, the group discovers how to work together as they go about setting and achieving goals. Finally, in the Adjourning stage, the group begins closure to their work and sets about transitioning to new roles.

It is important for advisors, supervisors, and student leaders to determine how best to integrate these methods into their organizations. For some, it may be a guided discussion over several meetings; others may already have an established comfort level with a group that allows them to begin using these tools immediately. Either way, advisors and supervisors need to understand that buy-in does not happen overnight. Instead, with patience, perseverance, and guided practice, learning can become ingrained in the environment of the organization, allowing students to grow beyond their perceived abilities.

Advisors should also be aware of learning styles—their own and those of the students with whom they work. Some people are visual learners, while others prefer auditory input or need to work with their hands for best results (VARK: A Guide to Learning Styles, 2011). Students may have preferences in how they learn. Rather than taking a cookie-cutter approach, the advisor has the responsibility to remove barriers in the learning environment to provide the best situation for success. The advisor does not have to be the expert in every area, but, as a good role model, the advisor should be committed to lifelong learning.

The Organization Cycle

Integrating learning into the culture of an organization can have an overwhelmingly positive impact on everyone involved. For example, since 2005, a freshman service organization at Texas A&M University has been using tools to intentionally document student learning. During this time span, the group has grown from infancy into maturity, and unlike most groups traversing these cycles, the organization has continued growing and developing without regressing back to the beginning.

When a group's advisor or supervisor incorporates student learning into the organization and documents the process, the student leaders begin to see an even greater value in their work, and they also more clearly see the bigger picture. This clarity of focus allows the students to focus on the goals for their group *and* also to spend time on their own self-development. Furthermore, student-focused learning will also allow group and organization leaders to work with their advisors and supervisors to create an atmosphere where peer-to-peer development can take place. When students focus on their organization's goals, concentrate on their own development, and assist their peers along their own growth paths, a learning atmosphere has truly been created.

Conclusion

The integration of learning into campus activities and student employment opportunities is not something that will simply happen overnight. This process needs to be intentional and shared widely with personnel across campus. Advisors and supervisors must act alongside their students to determine the roles each party will play within the organization. Everyone involved must work together to determine the part each will play in the process of integrating learning into the out-of-class student experience. To start, it is essential to have a guided discussion and evaluation of an organization's climate in order to examine the readiness of the group to begin the process.

Most important, the advisor and student leader must choose the path that works best for them and their respective organization(s). This process is similar to building a house: The advisor/supervisor pours the slab and sets a foundation to build on; the students then make the experience unique, depending on their wants and needs as a group. The floor plan, amenities, and wall color may change from year to year, but grounding the foundation in learning is up to the advisor/supervisor and can lead to a successful experience for all.

Questions for Reflection

1. How would you categorize the maturity of the student organization with which you work most closely? What are some ways in which you could assist in moving it toward organizational maturity?

2. Think about the last few conversations you have had with students. What could you have said to make the discussion more learning centered?

3. If you are an advisor, how would you describe the climate and environment of the student organization(s)?

4. If you are a supervisor of advisors, what conversations have you had with the advisors about creating and documenting a learning environment?

5. How would you begin a conversation about change with the chief student leader of the organization(s) you advise? How can this lead to the positive change that can occur when integrating learning into the student leader experience?

References

Allen, K. (1981). Choosing the effective advising style. *Programming Magazine, 16* (1), 34–37.

American College Personnel Association (ACPA) and National Association of Student Personnel Administrators (NASPA). (2010). *Professional competency areas for student affairs practitioners.* Retrieved from http://www.naspa.org/programs/prodev/Professional_Competencies.pdf

Baida, A. (2009). *Student leader learning outcomes: Rubric selection aid for organization advisors.* Retrieved from https://dsacms.tamu.edu/sites/sllo.tamu.edu/files/Choosing%20a%20Rubric.doc

Baxter Magolda, M. B., & King, P. M. (2008). Toward reflective conversations: An advising approach that promotes self-authorship. *Peer Review, 10*(1), 8–11.

Dunkel, N., & Schuh, J. (1998). *Advising student groups and organizations.* San Francisco, CA: Jossey-Bass.

Keeling, P. (Ed.). (2004). *Learning reconsidered: A campus-wide focus on the student experience.* Washington, DC: American College Personnel Association and National Association of Student Personnel Administrators.

Keeling, P. (Ed.). (2006). *Learning reconsidered 2: A practical guide to implementing a campus-wide focus on the student experience.* Washington, DC: American College Personnel Association and National Association of Student Personnel Administrators.

Komives, S. R., Lucas, N., & McMahon, T. R. (2007). *Exploring leadership for college students who want to make a difference* (2nd ed.). San Francisco, CA: Jossey-Bass.

Tuckman, B. W., & Jensen, M. C. (1977). Stages of small group development revisited. *Group and Organizational Studies, 2*(4), 419–426.

VARK: A Guide to Learning Styles. (2011). *The VARK Questionnaire.* Retrieved from http://www.vark-learn.com/english/page.asp?p=questionnaire

Whitt, E. J. (2006, January–February). Are all of your educators educating? *About Campus, 10*(6), 2–9.

DETERMINING THE ADVISOR ROLE

Directions: Check off your level of agreement for each of the following advisor roles:

In performing the role of advisor, I believe that an advisor should:	STRONGLY AGREE	AGREE	NO OPINION	DISAGREE	STRONGLY DISAGREE
Exhibit active listening skills and provide feedback accordingly					
Establish rapport with student executives					
Establish rapport with student members					
Facilitate reflection activities to create meaningful experience					
Understand and use appropriate nonverbal communication					
Pursue multiple objectives in conversations with students					
Facilitate problem solving					
Facilitate individual decision making					
Facilitate group decision making					
Facilitate individual goal setting					
Facilitate group goal setting					
Serve as a reference point for students (i.e., recommending resources, campus partners, funding sources, etc.)					
General Advising Roles					
Be an educator/trainer of leadership and organizational skills					
Be a developer of student volunteers					
Be an educator of program philosophy and program skills					

Be an attendee at events					
Be a doer of student programs					
Be a coordinator/advocate for a balanced student program					
Provide continuity between years					
Be a developer/planner of new programs					
Be held responsible for program failure					
Based on Institutional Goals/Practices (this section may vary)					

Note. Adapted from *Professional Competency Areas for Student Affairs Practitioners.* Copyright © 2010 by the American College Personnel Association and the National Association of Student Personnel Administrators. Reproduced with permission.

ACTIVITIES THAT HELP IDENTIFY ADVISOR AND SUPERVISOR EXPECTATIONS

The following activities may be carried out by the advisor/supervisor or head student leader of the student organizations. Some are focused on building rapport and establishing relationships with student groups before embarking on this journey, while others are rooted in the integration of learning in the cocurricular environment.

Activity #1: Setting Expectations

For use with: Individual students at the beginning of the year to establish rapport and set expectations.

Recommended time: This can be a 5-minute activity at a student leader retreat.

Organization stage: May be used with organizations in Infancy, Adolescence, Young Adulthood, or Maturity.

Instructions:

1. Student advisor distributes notecards.
2. Students are asked to respond to the following questions:
    - What is one expectation you have of me [the advisor] this year?
    - What is one expectation you have of yourself this year?
3. Advisor collects the cards and does periodic check-ins with student leaders throughout the year.
4. The expectations of self can be used as prompts during student exit interviews. At the end of the experience, or throughout the year, the advisor can analyze the response to develop themes, commonalities, areas of growth, or challenges. This can become part of a larger picture of student learning assessment.

Activity #2: Inbox Activity

For use with: Organization leaders that need help with writing skills.
Pair with: Written Communication Outcomes and Written Communication Rubric (see Appendices E and F).
Organization stage: May be used with organizations in Infancy, Adolescence, Young Adulthood, or Maturity.
Advisor's role: Provide feedback to students in terms of written communication, critical thinking, problem solving, and professionalism. This is an opportunity to help students reflect on their priorities and their role in representing the organization or department.

Instructions:

As a student leader, you will periodically receive e-mails from people ranging from parents to students to university officials. Part of your job is to respond adequately and appropriately to these e-mails, representing not only yourself but also your organization and university. This activity aims to serve as practice not only in responding to e-mails, but also in prioritizing your responses.

Assume that you are John Smith, president of the senior class. You have not been able to check your e-mail for 24 hours, and when you arrive to your desk on Monday morning, you have five e-mails in your inbox. You must respond to these e-mails in order as if you were responding directly to the person that sent you the request, question, or inquiry. For purposes of this exercise, you may write all responses in one e-mail, identifying the order in which you would send the responses.

The e-mails in your inbox are as follows:

John,

I am writing this in regard to your last economics test. A student approached me stating that you were sharing answers with your neighbors throughout the exam. I am giving you the benefit of the doubt, as we have an established relationship; however, I would like you to set up a meeting with me as soon as possible to discuss. Please call my assistant, Joshua, at 555-1234 at your earliest convenience.

Please respond with your reaction to these allegations so that I can be prepared for our meeting.

Jill Johnson, PhD
Associate Professor
College of Economics

B.

My son Jim was just accepted into this organization. He notified me that he needs to attend a retreat this Friday night. My husband and I were planning on coming into town to drop off his TV this Friday. I was wondering what the details of the retreat are, so that we can plan around it in order to get Jim's TV to him.

Thanks,

Rhonda Thompson

C.

To Whom It May Concern:

My name is Sue Masters, and I am a teacher at Parkview High School. Every year we host a "Get Involved Fair" for our students, encouraging them to focus on school pride. We are hoping that someone from your organization would be able to come speak to our students about why they chose to get involved at AU and what impact they have had on the school through their involvement. The fair is on October 27 from 1 p.m. to 3 p.m. Please let me know if you or someone else can attend.

Thanks,

Mrs. Sue Masters
Parkview High School

D.

To Whom It May Concern:

I recently registered for the Senior Class Real World Conference and want to know a little more about what to expect to prepare myself. The specific sessions I signed up for include résumé writing, professional interview skills, and the etiquette dinner. Am I supposed to bring a copy of my personal résumé? Will we get one-on-one attention to reformat this document? What will the professional interview be like? What should I wear to the dinner?

Thanks so much for your response,

Ryan Radley

E.

John,

The monthly student leader meeting is quickly approaching, and we have not received your outline for the senior class presentation. Please e-mail your notes to my assistant by Wednesday at 8 a.m. so that I can give you feedback.

Regards,

Dr. Emersyn
President
AU

Activity #3: Exit Interview

(Adapted from Extended Orientation Director Interviews at Texas A&M University)

For use with: Individual student leaders at the end of their tenure.
Organization stage: May be used with organizations in Infancy, Adolescence, Young Adulthood, or Maturity.

Instructions:

Ideally, long before exit interviews are conducted, an intentional learning plan based on a theory or model has been presented to the students and implemented throughout the leadership or job experience. Questions should be grounded in the outcomes the organization created at the beginning of the year. Depending on the number of interviews completed, the advisor may want to complete a formal content analysis to determine themes, document growth, and determine what training strategies can be used in the future to enhance the learning for the next generation of students.

Format:

Each student should be given the set of questions prior to the final meeting. Depending on the nature of the questions and preference of the student, advisors may be present during the interview. If not, another student advisor will be identified to facilitate the discussion.

Questions:

1. What did you learn from your experience (skills, talents, abilities, etc.)?
2. Did you meet the expectations you set for yourself this year? Why or why not?
3. What would you define as your greatest personal accomplishment? Greatest organizational accomplishment?
4. What was the greatest struggle you faced as a student leader? What was the greatest struggle of your student organization? How did you overcome these struggles?
5. What is one skill you were able to develop through your student leader role? How will you use this skill (and others) in your next step (e.g., student position, job search, career, etc.)?
6. What role did your advisor play within your organization? Do you feel he or she appropriately supported you and your organization?

7. How do you feel the department supported your student organization? What would you like to see improved for future years?

8. What recommendations would you make for next year's student executive staff?

APPENDIX E
WRITTEN COMMUNICATION OUTCOMES

Definition Of Written Communication:

Writing is the representation of language in a textual medium through the use of a set of signs or symbols (known as a writing system). (Taken directly from: http://en.wikipedia.org/wiki/Written_communication)

Outcomes:

Students will be able to:
- Effectively communicate through the written word for a wide variety of purposes and audiences
- Accurately convey the intent of their message when writing
- Structure written communication that is clear, logical, and easy to follow
- Use correct mechanics such as grammar, spelling, and punctuation
- Select and incorporate appropriate supporting materials
- Effectively adjust their writing styles to appropriately address the audience

Other Useful Rubrics Related to This Topic:

Oral Communication, Interpersonal Communication

Resources:

- Writing Center at Texas A&M University (http://writingcenter.tamu.edu)
  ⇨ Provides handouts, webliography of online resources, consultant services, freelance editors, workshops

- Writing Skills: Before You Write It Down, Know This (http://www.mindtools.com/CommSkll/WritingSkills.htm)
- The OWL (Online Writing Lab) at Purdue University
    - ⇨ Effective Workplace Writing (http://owl.english.purdue.edu/owl/resource/624/01)
    - ⇨ Audience Analysis Overview (http://owl.english.purdue.edu/owl/resource/629/01)
    - ⇨ Introduction to Pre-Writing (http://owl.english.purdue.edu/owl/resource/673/01)
    - ⇨ Email Etiquette (http://owl.english.purdue.edu/owl/resource/636/01)
    - ⇨ Writing the Basic Business Letter (http://owl.english.purdue.edu/owl/resource/653/01)
    - ⇨ Memo Writing (http://owl.english.purdue.edu/owl/resource/590/01)
    - ⇨ Tone in Business Writing (http://owl.english.purdue.edu/owl/resource/652/01)
    - ⇨ Paragraphs and Paragraphing (http://owl.english.purdue.edu/owl/resource/606/01)
    - ⇨ Using Appropriate Language (http://owl.english.purdue.edu/owl/resource/608/01)

AggiEfolio Competencies That This Rubric Addresses:

Cluster 1: Problem Solving and Thinking Skillfully
- Observation Skills
- Analyzing Critical Data

Cluster 2: Communicating Effectively
- Basic Communication Skills
- Written Communication Skills
- Technical Writing Skills

Cluster 6: Managing Resources
- Managing Self

Note. Adapted from *Written Communication Outcomes Student Leader Learning Outcomes (SLLO) Project.* Copyright © 2008 by Student Life Studies, Texas A&M University. Reproduced with permission.

WRITTEN COMMUNICATION RUBRIC

Name of Student:		Date Completed:			
WRITTEN COMMUNICATION OUTCOMES	**NOVICE**	**TRANSITION**	**INTERMEDIATE**	**TRANSITION**	**ADVANCED**
	Awareness or Base-level Knowledge	From Novice to Intermediate	Apply the Concept Somewhat	From Intermediate to Advanced	Intentional and Effective Application
Clarity	Rarely provides a clear main idea supported by sufficient details.		Occasionally provides a clear main idea supported by sufficient details.		Consistently provides a clear main idea supported by rich, vivid, and powerful details.
Purpose	Does not exhibit the ability to identify different purposes and types of communication.		Can occasionally identify and adjust to specific purposes of communication (e.g., entertain, inspire, motivate, understanding, accurate recall, persuasion, decision making).		Can consistently identify and adjust to specific purposes of communication (e.g., entertain, inspire, motivate, understanding, accurate recall, persuasion, decision making).

Structure	Written work has weak beginning, development, and conclusion. Main idea is not clear. Paragraphs and transitions have persistent errors.		Written work has adequate beginning, development, and conclusion. Main idea is vague or does not match with the argument. Paragraphs and transitions are adequate.		Written work has clear and appropriate beginning, development, and conclusion. Main idea is clearly communicated. Paragraphs and transitions are clear and appropriate.
Content	Written work does not adequately address the topic. Assumptions or claims are not supported by evidence.		Written work is sufficient to cover the topic. Assumptions or claims are weakly supported by evidence.		Written work provides in-depth coverage of the topic. Assumptions or claims are clearly supported by evidence.
Mechanics	Written work has persistent errors in word selection and use, sentence structure, spelling, punctuation, and/or capitalization.		Written work has occasional errors in word selection and use, sentence structure, spelling, punctuation, and/or capitalization.		Written work is relatively free of errors in word selection and use, sentence structure, spelling, punctuation, and/or capitalization.
Context	Does not select the correct and appropriate method in which to communicate written information. Is not aware of the needs of the audience.		Occasionally selects the correct and appropriate method in which to communicate written information. Is aware of some of the needs of the audience and tries to meet them but misses other needs.		Consistently selects the correct and appropriate method in which to communicate written information. Is fully aware of the needs of the audience and tries to meet those needs.

COMMENTS:

Note. Adapted from *Written Communication Rubric Student Leader Learning Outcomes (SLLO) Project.* Copyright © 2008 by Student Life Studies, Texas A&M University. Reproduced with permission.

CHAPTER 6

THE STUDENT LEARNING FOCUSED ADVISOR/SUPERVISOR

Krista Jorge Bailey

I f you were to ask most student affairs professionals if they wanted their students to learn from their involvement experiences, the answer would be a resounding "Yes!" None of us want our students to go through an experience just for the sake of the experience. However, when we were in graduate school, most of our programs did not focus on teaching staff to be educators. We learned student development theory and how to assist students with a number of issues, but there were very few programs that focused on student learning.

The average advisor or supervisor provides support to their student organizations and staff. Student organization advisors may attend an occasional meeting or even every meeting. They support the students' programs and events and help them fulfill their organizational mission and purpose. Student assistant supervisors provide appropriate supervision, which may include feedback and training, but it is unrealistic to think that advisors and supervisors will be around all the time. They support students, but they may miss an opportunity to truly engage students in the learning experience if they do not actively focus on student learning. *Learning Reconsidered* (Keeling, 2004) defined learning as a "complex, holistic, multi-centric activity that occurs throughout and across the college experience" (p. 5). Learning occurs throughout the college experience, and as student affairs professionals, it is our responsibility to facilitate learning in our areas.

The student learning focused advisor and/or supervisor is someone who values student learning, values the documentation of student learning, and actually documents the learning that occurs within the scope of his or her responsibilities. Student learning focused advisors maximize their interactions with students to support holistic learning. For example, a student learning focused advisor/supervisor asks individual students to develop a learning contract at the beginning of the year, outlining what he or she wants to learn through the involvement experience. The advisor then meets with the student on a regular basis to provide feedback on the student's learning and help him or her identify areas of growth and areas of strength. At the end of the experience, the student is able to articulate and demonstrate the learning that has resulted.

This chapter will discuss a number of factors related to implementing a student learning focused approach that extends beyond the individual and encompasses the organizational culture. It is not enough for staff members to want to be student learning focused; the organizational culture and processes must support, encourage, and develop the skills needed to pursue these efforts. As you continue to read this chapter, consider the following questions:

1. What is your supervisory style?
2. Do you value student learning?
3. Do you document student learning?
4. Do you have conversations with students about what they are learning?
5. What does your organization say about student learning?
6. How are you supported in your student learning efforts?

Organizations would be wise to consider how the culture supports or discourages staff to be focused on student learning. There are a number of different strategies organizations can use to support this type of culture including learning organizations, training, professional development, effective supervision, and position descriptions and expectations. Organizations that are successful in supporting student learning not only promote the efforts but also have accountability measures in place to sustain the efforts. Each of these strategies will be discussed in the remainder of this chapter.

Organizational Culture

Schein (1990) defined organizational culture as:

> A pattern of basic assumptions, invented, discovered, or developed by a given group, as it learns to cope with its problems of external adaptation and internal integration, that has worked well enough to be considered valid and, therefore is to be taught to new members as the correct way to perceive, think, and feel in relation to those problems. (p. 111)

It is important to understand the organizational culture when considering student learning because it provides a framework in which to understand how student learning is encouraged or discouraged. Organizational culture can be manifested in three levels: "(a) observable artifacts, (b) values, and (c) basic underlying assumptions" (Schein, 1990, p. 111).

When considering organizational culture, there are multiple layers within an institution that could be defined as an organization. For example, let's consider the Department of Student Activities at a large university. The individual department will have a culture that will dictate how staff should behave and perform and what they should value. That department is part of a larger Division of Student Affairs, which will have norms and values based on the mission and purpose. Finally, the division is a part of the university. Ideally the mission, purpose, and values will be aligned among all three units, but that is not always the case. Understanding the reward system, both intrinsic and extrinsic, at the various organizational levels can assist with understanding how student learning is or is not supported. Organizational cultures exist on all campuses and are influenced by all the different stakeholders. For example, a community college's organizational culture may be influenced by the student population and the mission and purpose of the college. Cultures differ from one organization to another, but all shape what employees view as valued and important. King and Baxter Magolda (2011) stated:

> Student learning in postsecondary education involves more than the acquisition of knowledge and skills; it also includes developing a frame of mind that allows students to put their knowledge in perspective; to understand the sources of their beliefs and values; and to establish a sense of self that enables them to participate effectively in a variety of personal, occupational, and community contexts. (p. 207)

In order for this type of learning to occur, students need to seamlessly travel from one environment to the next that supports learning, and the organizational culture influences how students perceive this process.

As a practitioner, you can use the climate instrument presented in Chapter 5 to help determine the characteristics of your organizational culture. You may determine that organizational development and change is needed to shift the organization's culture from an old paradigm to one focused on student development.

Organization Development and Organizational Change

Beckhard (2006) defined organization development as "an effort, planned organization-wide, and managed from the top to increase organization effectiveness and health through planned interventions in the organization's 'processes,' using behavioral science knowledge" (p. 3). Organization development is an intentional effort designed to make structured and predetermined changes to an organization. In theory, organization development is an excellent opportunity to create a healthy, well-functioning organization; however, there are multiple conditions that must be present for the outcomes of an organization development plan to be achieved as designed. These conditions are tied to the staff of the organization and human nature (for example, fear of change may inhibit the positive efforts of organization development).

Organization development is an intentional effort designed to make structured and predetermined changes to an organization (Beckhard, 2006). In order for the effects of organization development to be as successful as possible, the top management must be invested and have a sense of shared responsibility, vision, and desired outcomes. Becoming a student learning focused organization is not a quick transition. There must be buy-in from multiple levels, as well as significant time to see results. Organizational change theory can assist in developing a plan to implement change.

Kotter (2006) described an eight-step change process that accounts for the multiple steps and stages needed to successfully implement organizational change:

1. Establish a sense of urgency.
2. Form a powerful guiding coalition.
3. Create a vision.
4. Communicate the vision.
5. Empower others to act on the vision.
6. Plan for and create short-term wins.

7. Consolidate improvements and produce still more change.
8. Institutionalize new approaches. (p. 243)

Depending on your role in the organization, you may have a different function during each of these steps. Consider your role and the power you have to influence change. This chapter discusses each step of Kotter's change model and tools to implement student learning within each step. There is a broad continuum of situations, from institutions that support student learning and have embedded it into all of their work to institutions that do not consider the learning that occurs in their student affairs programs and activities. Each tool presented in the context of this change model can be used independently, depending on the needs of the institution. In Chapter 8, this change model will be applied as a case study to demonstrate how a university progressed through the steps.

Establish a Sense of Urgency

If people do not understand why change is needed, they are less likely to want to change. There must be an urgent and immediate need for change and champions to support the change efforts (Kotter, 2006). For student learning, there are a number of tools available to create a sense of urgency on campus. The Liberal Education and America's Promise (LEAP) project from the Association of American Colleges and Universities (AAC&U) provides resources for colleges and universities to focus on student learning and promotes learning outcomes, high-impact educational practices, authentic assessments, and inclusive excellence (AAC&U, 2011). Many of the recommended practices from LEAP are applicable to student affairs and can be used to demonstrate the significant learning that occurs outside the classroom. *Learning Reconsidered* (Keeling, 2004) and *Learning Reconsidered 2* (Keeling, 2006) are publications from the American College Personnel Association (ACPA) and the National Association of Student Personnel Administrators (NASPA) that can be used to create a sense of urgency related to student learning. Many institutions, such as Texas A&M University, have developed a set of learning outcomes as part of an academic master plan for their different student populations (Texas A&M University, 2009). The National Institute for Learning Outcomes Assessment (2011) highlights university websites that communicate outcomes well, provide easy navigation, and express outcomes assessment in creative or interesting ways. Some of the institutions featured are Walden University, Juniata College, Northern Arizona University, and Joliet Junior College. Although the institutions differ, they have all committed to learning outcomes assessment. As described in Chapter 5, many staff members think documenting student learning means more work; creating a sense of urgency gives staff the opportunity to see beyond the fear.

Form a Powerful Guiding Coalition

This group needs to have power to lead the change effort but does not have to be within the normal hierarchy (Kotter, 2006). The group should have a shared commitment to excellence and be willing and able to work as a team (Kotter, 2006). One strategy for developing a powerful guiding coalition is to use a learning organization. Senge (2006) defined a learning organization as:

> Organizations where people continually expand their capacity to create the results they truly desire, where new and expansive patterns of thinking are nurtured, where collective aspiration is set free, and where people are continually learning to see the whole together. (p. 3)

A learning organization can be a department, a division, a university, or even a committee. Allowing the definition to be applied to a number of contexts will allow the principles to be easily adopted.

In *The Fifth Discipline Fieldbook*, Senge, Kleiner, Roberts, Ross, and Smith (1994) described learning organizations as being based upon five learning disciplines: personal mastery, mental models, shared vision, team learning, and systems thinking. Personal mastery is "learning to expand our personal capacity" (Senge et al., 1994, p. 6). As staff members who want to be more student learning focused, we need to be able to evaluate our own set of skills and areas of growth. Mental models describe how we see the world (Senge et al., 1994) and what our paradigms are toward our work. Focusing on student learning may be natural and easy for some staff members and more of a challenge for others. As student affairs personnel, we need to be able to identify our mental models and evaluate how they affect our work.

A shared vision is a commitment within the group toward the same set of goals and objectives (Senge et al., 1994). Team learning is "transforming conversational and collective thinking skills, so that groups of people can reliably develop intelligence and ability greater than the sum of the individual members' talents (Senge et al., 1994, p. 6). A learning organization focusing on student learning allows staff to learn from one another in order to enrich and enhance the student experience. A learning organization allows boundaries to be crossed and provides opportunities for staff from different functional areas and varying years of experience. The fifth learning discipline for learning organizations, systems thinking, is an ability to look at the larger systems and processes that are present in the organization (Senge et al., 1994). Student learning does not happen in a vacuum and should be reinforced across the institution. Systems thinking allows for an understanding of the processes that shape the learning environment. A learning organization is one strategy for building a powerful guiding coalition, but it is not the only strategy for developing a strong group of individuals willing to lead the initiative.

Create a Vision

Kotter (2006) stated, "A vision says something that helps clarify the direction in which an organization needs to move" (p. 244). The vision should be easily communicated and should create buy-in to the project by others (Kotter, 2006). Once the vision is established, strategies must be developed to achieve that vision (Kotter, 2006). For example, an institution may say it wants to enrich the student learning experience on its campus. What does that mean? How is it going to happen? Who is going to be involved? These questions need to be answered because the next step is communicating the vision. In order for the vision to be effective, it needs to speak to the audience and be clearly articulated for the audience to understand. Staff need to be able to see themselves and their work in the vision statement, as well as how they could be key contributors to reaching the vision. The vision may come from a number of sources: the institution, the department, or a group within the division.

Communicate the Vision

A vision is only as strong as the people who are embracing its concepts. The vision needs to communicate a message that seems possible to the receivers, and it needs to become part of the day-to-day conversations (Kotter, 2006). It must be communicated not only with words but also through deeds (Kotter, 2006). For example, if a vice president for student affairs charged the division with creating a set of learning outcomes for every program, he or she would need to put in place accountability measures to demonstrate the value of those initiatives, or talk about the student learning that is being reported. The vision may need to be shared up and down, and with each group, appropriate skills and knowledge may be needed to help move the individual and organization toward the desired behaviors of the vision.

Empower Others to Act on the Vision

Once people begin to see themselves and their work as part of the organization's vision, they must be empowered to act. This involves removing obstacles, supporting risk taking, and trying new ideas (Kotter, 2006). This step of the change process is where organizations can focus significant time and energy to promote student learning. The supervisor should assess the knowledge and skills of the staff advisors and supervisors and decide whether these levels need to be enhanced to provide and measure the learning opportunities available for students. Harper (2011) called for student affairs professionals to become intentional in their efforts to foster an environment for student learning. He said that "perhaps most important, intentionality demands seeing oneself as an educator rather than a practitioner, staff member, advisor, director, or some other title commonly assigned to those responsible for student learning and development outside the classroom" (p. 291). Effective supervision, staff orientation, training, and professional development are all tools to empower others to act on the vision and become intentional educators. Each of these topics will be discussed below.

Effective supervision. Advisors and student assistant supervisors may be supervised by mid-level managers who may not work with students directly and therefore may not be as in touch with the need for student learning. The supervision the advisors and student assistant supervisors receive is critical. Tull (2006) noted, "[S]taff supervision is one of the most complex activities for which organizational leaders are responsible, and certain skills and knowledge about staff development are required for effective supervision" (p. 465). Supervisors must understand the organizational expectations for student learning and how to support their staff members who are working directly with the students. Hirt and Strayhorn (2011) said it best when they wrote, "[S]upervision entails a relationship between manager and staff member that aims to facilitate the attainment of both organizational and institutional objectives" (p. 374).

Effective supervision for student learning is critical to moving the student learning vision forward. For some staff members, implementing a learning contract or a skill rubric with a student may be daunting and challenging. Supervisory support can also be demonstrated in actions. Supervisors have the ability to make student learning a priority, to ask staff about their initiatives at regular meetings, and to discuss efforts and successes during performance evaluations. To reinforce the importance of the issue, supervisors can include student learning in position descriptions and staff expectations, a practice that will also allow supervisors to evaluate staff on their student learning efforts, thereby reinforcing the organizational accountability for the implementation. Without a student learning focused supervisor, some staff members may not see the value of the approach and therefore not engage in activities that promote student learning with their students. Fundamentally, supervisors must understand how to implement student learning initiatives. A supervisor who does not have the basic knowledge can seek training to understand the principles. By seeking training, the supervisor will be reinforcing the importance of the vision, and acting as a role model for his or her staff on the value of professional development.

Orientation and training. If departmental or organizational governing documents support student learning, the focus on that approach is reinforced. And there should be congruence between governing documents and the words and actions of organizational leaders. The organizational expectations must be shared with new staff, and training must be provided to ensure continued growth and development of staff members. Orientation programs provide the knowledge and skills necessary for staff members to be effective in their positions (Hirt & Strayhorn, 2011).

For student learning, orientation can occur in two forms. Organizations that are changing and shifting their paradigm toward student learning can offer orientation sessions to all staff as a way to provide them with the foundational knowledge needed to be successful. The orientation should be designed to best meet the needs of the audience and be based on instructional design principles, such as conducting a needs assessment, writing performance objectives, specifying instructional strategies, etc. (Rothwell & Kazanas, 1998). Table 1 shows an example of an agenda for a 2011 student learning orientation used for the Student Leader Learning Outcomes (SLLO) project at Texas A&M University. This orientation tool can also be a vehicle for communicating the vision.

Table 1

Student Learning Orientation Schedule Example

Module	Instruction	Learning Outcomes	Materials
Welcome and introduction	• Introduction of participants • Housekeeping items		• Nametags • SLLO pens
Know SLLO	• Presentation of SLLO • Student learning outcomes activity	Participants will be able to articulate: • The history of the SLLO Project • The purpose of SLLO • The importance of student learning in the cocurricular environment	• Slides • Documents
Stocking your SLLO toolkit	• Presentation of SLLO tools • Activity with SLLO tools	Participants will be able to: • Implement tools when working with students • Assist students in translating experience to learning • Create space for student learning opportunities • Have tools to be able to integrate SLLO into work • Know how to measure student learning and integrate the practice of measuring student learning into their work	• Slides • Example tools

Empower SLLO	• Overview of self-authorship • Activity with self-authorship tool	Participants will be able to: • Talk to students about their learning • Empower students to engage in their own learning • Communicate organizational need and purpose • Identify where a student is developmentally with regard to student learning	• Slides
Life with SLLO	• Presentation of opportunities available for SLLO • Action planning • Evaluation	Participants will: • Know how to continue involvement with SLLO • Know resources that are available • Develop an action plan based on their self-assessment of skill competence	• Calendar • Action plan

The second type of orientation is for all new staff members. This can be helpful for organizations with a rich culture of student learning. The orientation program would provide an overview of expectations related to student learning and skills necessary to be successful. The orientation process is a critical time to ensure all new staff understand the importance of student learning in their work.

A great orientation program is not sufficient; continued training and development is needed to ensure staff have the appropriate knowledge, skills, and abilities to be successful in their roles. Hirt and Strayhorn (2011) stated, "[S]taff development involves purposefully designed, multi-faceted activities that enable staff members to address gaps in their knowledge and to gain new skills that promote individual growth and institutional advancement" (p. 374). Staff development can take the form of training. Noe (2008) defined training as "a planned effort by a company to facilitate employees' learning or job-related competencies" (p. 4). Training is designed to expand employees' competencies and prepare them to execute tasks and processes related to a position. Training programs should be developed that will meet the needs of multiple learning styles. According to Downey and Zeltmann (2009), "It is not enough in today's training environment to focus solely on skills training; an individual's underlying motivation to learn is a critical aspect in successful training efforts" (p. 98).

A well-designed training program will help institutions develop intentional educators. Whitt (2006) reinforced the need for competent professionals, noting, "Any institution that wishes to emphasize student achievement, satisfaction, persistence, and learning must have competent student affairs professionals who contribute to the academic mission of the institution in ways that help students and the institution realize their goals" (p. 2). The knowledge, skills, and abilities needed to implement the student learning plan for the organization must be identified.

The training program should be developed in relation to these specifics in order to prepare staff to infuse student learning in their work. For example, if students are going to be asked to write learning contracts, the staff member will need to understand how to write a learning plan, how to measure goals and objectives, and how to help students reflect on their experiences and articulate their learning. If staff members are being asked to measure the learning in their programs, they will need to be able to write learning outcomes and develop assessment tools to measure those learning outcomes. Many staff members know how to write learning outcomes or how to develop a learning contract with students, but they do not know how to document the learning, which is key. Often, specific training is needed on what to do with the information collected. The plan must be customized to the individual organization. Harper (2011) discussed the shift from the term extracurricular to cocurricular to define student's learning outside of the classroom, but contended that student affairs professionals often did not know how to structure a meaningful learning curriculum. Therefore, it is the responsibility of the organization to provide training to staff. Table 2 includes a list of knowledge, skills, and abilities that are frequently required to implement student learning initiatives (M. Langford, R. Rahn, S. Jaks, & A. Donaldson, personal communication, September 16, 2011).

Table 2

Knowledge, Skills, and Abilities for Student Learning

Knowledge	Skills	Abilities/Traits
• Awareness of self in relation to student learning initiatives • Awareness of student learning tools available at institution • Student development theory • Organizational development theory • Student learning theory and principles	• Cultivate relationships with students and build support networks with staff • Evaluation and assessment skills • Feedback delivery skills	• Resilience to try to incorporate learning regardless of obstacles • Flexibility and perseverance • Motivation and commitment to student learning

Professional development. Student learning is not a one-stop shop where you can learn everything you need to know in one training. Professional development is a focus on continuous learning and development (Kruger, 2000). The field of student learning is always evolving, and it is important for staff members to stay current. Professional development is one tool to help staff continue to develop and grow. Hirt and Strayhorn (2011) wrote that "practitioners become highly productive, effective administrators through professional development" (p. 380). Professional development opportunities are nearly limitless. There are a number of conferences and organizations focused on leadership, such as the International Leadership Association or the Association of Leadership Educators. NASPA and ACPA have subgroups focused on leadership and assessment, such as the NASPA Student Leadership Programs Knowledge Community. These organizations host national conferences, webinars, and subgroups on specialized topics and publications that often feature information on student learning.

The strategies mentioned above help organizations to empower staff to act on the vision. If staff members do not act, take risks, and remove structures that impede student learning, the initiatives will not become embedded within the organizational culture.

Plan for and create short-term wins. Kotter (2006) called for the acknowledgement and celebration of short-term wins after obstacles that impede organizational change are removed. Celebration is a critical component of sustaining a student learning focus. Implementing student learning is not easy; there will be ups and downs. Some students will be very receptive and others will not want to participate or engage in the learning. Some staff members will naturally be willing to try new things or have a natural inclination for student learning. Other staff members may be challenged by approaching their work from a different paradigm. Learning to recognize and celebrate the short-term wins will help maintain energy around the project and will increase the number of staff interested in joining the efforts.

There are multiple strategies available for celebrating short-term wins. They should be developed based on what motivates staff on your campus. Three examples of strategies are highlighting staff members, telling the student's story, and rewarding student learning focused staff. Staff members who are working on implementing student learning can be recognized at department or division meetings. The stories of students who have benefited from student learning initiatives can be shared. There are numerous avenues for sharing this information including meetings, newsletters, and websites. At times, the student voice is the most powerful voice to create energy toward a student learning project. Staff could be rewarded for their student learning initiatives, for example, by receiving monetary awards, grants for programs, or an annual award for student learning efforts. Regardless of the strategy, short-term wins will help the organizational change effort to continue to advance.

Consolidate improvements and produce still more change. Kotter (2006) urged organizations to not declare a victory too soon; short-term wins must be celebrated and used to create more change. Organizations will not advance their student learning initiatives if they only develop a handful of staff who have implemented student learning and then rely on those staff members to continue the project. Those areas and groups may continue to grow and develop their approach to student learning, but it will not become part of the system. There is a high level of staff turnover in student affairs, and in order for student learning to become part of the organizational culture, it must be institutionalized beyond individual staff members.

Institutionalize new approaches. In order to fully support and encourage staff to be student learning focused, student learning must become a valued part of the organizational culture. Kotter (2006) described two factors that are important to institutionalizing the organizational change. "The first is a conscious attempt to show people how the new approaches, behaviors, and attitudes have helped improve performance" (p. 250). What matters to your institution? Are evidence and data important? Are students' experiences important? Knowing what information will have the most impact will help you determine how to illustrate that performance has improved and that you are enhancing your ability to serve your students.

There are many ways in which staff can implement student learning initiatives that reinforce the institutionalization of a student learning focused approach. The Wabash National Study provides longitudinal research about teaching, student experiences, and institutional conditions that promote the development of students' critical thinking, moral reasoning, leadership toward social justice, well-being, interest in and engagement with diversity, and interest in deep intellectual work (Blaich & Wise, 2011). This research indicated several examples of good practices and conditions, including having faculty and staff who:

- Have a genuine interest in teaching and are interested in helping students grow in more than just academic areas
- Provide timely feedback
- Check to see if students learned the material before moving on to new material
- Design clear explanations of their course or program goals and requirements
- Develop organized classes and presentations
- Provide clear explanations of course goals and requirements
- Engage in high-quality nonclassroom interactions that influence students' growth, values, career aspirations, and interest in ideas

- Ensure that students work hard to prepare for their classes and are required to read and write a substantial amount of material
- Challenge students to analyze and synthesize information and make judgments about ideas, experiences, and theories
- Ask students to integrate ideas and information from different sources and to include diverse perspectives in their work
- Ask students to examine the strengths and weaknesses of their ideas and to understand someone else's view by imagining how an issue looks from his or her perspective (Blaich & Wise, 2011, p. 10)

All of us can undertake one or more of these good practices as student affairs professionals committed to providing students many learning and development opportunities.

Kotter's (2006) second important factor in institutionalizing change is "taking sufficient time to make sure that the next generation of top management really does personify the new approach" (p. 251). How are you selecting and training staff to have a student learning focused approach? In the staff selection process, how is student learning incorporated? What basic skills and knowledge related to student learning do staff members need in order to be successful candidates for positions? Answering these questions can help organizations ensure that new staff will perpetuate the organizational change efforts because they have become embedded into the organizational culture. Once staff are hired, they need to be trained in the values of the organization. As discussed above, new staff orientation is a venue for giving staff the necessary skills to implement student learning. It is also a venue for ensuring that the leadership and staff at all levels of the organization value student learning.

Conclusion

This chapter discussed a number of factors related to implementing a student learning focused approach from the framework of organizational culture. Organizations should evaluate how their culture supports or discourages staff to be focused on student learning. Once the culture has been evaluated, organizations can use a number of different strategies to support a student learning culture, including learning organizations, training and development, effective supervision, and position descriptions and expectations. Organizations that are successful in supporting student learning not only promote the efforts but also have accountability measures in place to sustain the efforts. These organizations enhance the learning experience for their students.

Questions for Reflection

1. Would you describe your organization as student learning focused? Why or why not?
2. How does the culture of your organization promote or impede student learning?
3. How do you prepare staff to be student learning focused?

References

Association of American Colleges and Universities (AAC&U). Liberal education and America's promise (LEAP). Retrieved from http://www.aacu.org/LEAP/index.cfm

Beckard, R. (2006). What is organization development? In J. V. Gallos (Ed.), *Organizational Development* (1ˢᵗ ed., pp. 3–12). San Francisco, CA: Jossey-Bass.

Blaich, C. F., & Wise, K. S. (2011, January). *From gathering to using assessment results: Lessons from the Wabash National Study* (NILOA Occasional Paper No. 8). Urbana, IL: University of Illinois and Indiana University, National Institute for Learning Outcomes Assessment.

Downey, J., & Zeltmann, S. (2009). The role of competence level in the self-efficacy-skills relationship: An empirical examination of the skill acquisition process and its implications for information technology training. *International Journal of Training and Development, 13*, 96–110.

Harper, S. R. (2011). Strategy and intentionality in practice. In J. H. Schuh, S. R. Jones, & S. R. Harper (Eds.), *Student services: A handbook for the profession* (5ᵗʰ ed., pp. 287–302). San Francisco, CA: Jossey-Bass.

Hirt, J. B., & Strayhorn, T. L. (2011). Staffing and supervision. In J. H. Schuh, S. R. Jones, & S. R. Harper (Eds.), *Student services: A handbook for the profession* (5ᵗʰ ed., pp. 372–384). San Francisco, CA: Jossey-Bass.

Keeling, R. P. (Ed.). (2004). *Learning reconsidered: A campus-wide focus on the student experience.* Washington, DC: American College Personnel Association and National Association of Student Personnel Administrators.

Keeling, R. P. (Ed.). (2006). *Learning reconsidered 2: A practical guide to implementing a campus-wide focus on the student experience.* Washington, DC: American College Personnel Association and National Association of Student Personnel Administrators.

King, P. M., & Baxter Magolda, M. B. (2011). Student learning. In J. H. Schuh, S. R. Jones, & S. R. Harper (Eds.), *Student services: A handbook for the profession* (5ᵗʰ ed., pp. 201–225). San Francisco, CA: Jossey-Bass.

Kotter, J. P. (2006). Leading change: Why transformation efforts fail. In J. V. Gallos

(Ed.), *Organizational Development* (1ˢᵗ ed., pp. 239–251). San Francisco, CA: Jossey-Bass.

Kruger, K. (2000). New alternatives for professional development. In M. J. Barr & M. K. Desler (Eds.), *The handbook of student affairs administration* (2ⁿᵈ ed., pp. 535–553). San Francisco, CA: Jossey-Bass.

National Institute for Learning Outcomes Assessment. (2011). Featured website. Retrieved from http://www.learningoutcomeassessment.org/FeaturedWebsite.html

Noe, R. A. (2008). *Employee training & development* (4th ed.). New York: McGraw-Hill.

Rothwell, W. J., & Kazanas, H. C. (1998). *Mastering the instructional design process* (2ⁿᵈ ed.). San Francisco, CA: Jossey–Bass.

Schein, E. H. (1990). Organizational culture. *American Psychologist, 45*(2), 109–119.

Senge, P. M. (2006). *The fifth discipline: The art and practice of the learning organization.* New York, NY: Doubleday.

Senge, P. M., Kleiner, A., Roberts, C., Ross, R. B., & Smith, B. J. (1994). *The fifth discipline fieldbook.* New York, NY: Doubleday.

Student Leader Learning Outcomes (SLLO). (2011). [Orientation schedule]. Unpublished raw data.

Texas A&M University. (2009). *Academic master plan.* Retrieved from http://provost.tamu.edu/initiatives/academic-master-plan/AMP_DRAFT_092409_MASTERrev.pdf

Tull, A. (2006). Synergistic supervision, job satisfaction, and intention to turnover of new professionals in student affairs. *Journal of College Student Development, 47*(4), 465–480.

Whitt, E. J. (2006, January/February). Are all of your educators educating? *About Campus*, 2–9.

CHAPTER 7

PROJECT ASSESSMENT
How Can We Improve Continually?

Sandi Osters

Chapter 3 dealt with the many different student affairs resources available to develop the student learning outcomes in higher education for which a large number of stakeholder groups demand evidence. Chapter 4 detailed multiple, creative ways for students to be involved in and see the results of their own learning in their cocurricular experiences and for advisors to offer and promote these opportunities. The challenge for many student affairs divisions—and specifically for the individual or office in the division or college charged with assessment responsibility—is to provide an understanding not only of what individual students are learning but also of how the cocurricular experience has specifically contributed to that learning. That challenge can be overwhelming because students' cocurricular experiences are as diverse as the varied departments, activities, and services that provide them.

This dilemma was underscored recently when a query on a student affairs assessment leaders' electronic mailing list asked, "How do you aggregate data about students' learning in their cocurricular experiences . . . when [institutional assessment offices] challenge us to aggregate the data in a way that it can be used as evidence for SACS [Southern Association of Colleges and Schools] accreditation as well as [a state higher education coordinating board]?" (S. Osters, personal communication, June 21, 2011). Two institutions responded with examples from their campuses, which will be detailed later in this chapter as case studies. But the response that possibly spoke for the majority of nonresponders said, "If you get it figured out I would be very appreciative as we have been asked to do that here. I have been trying to think about how to put it all together to make some sense of it as a whole and am also stuck" (R. Sanderson, personal communication, June 21, 2011).

This chapter will present an array of approaches—both tried and untried—that provide evidence of student learning in their cocurricular experiences. The chapter will investigate (a) showcasing student leaders in institutional assessment programs, (b) meta assessment of cocurricular outcomes through three case studies, and (c) student learning through the lens of student development theory. It will also touch on how to evaluate a program whose purpose is to assess student learning.

Institutional Assessment Programs

Overview

Many institutions are bound by the responsibility to provide evidence that students have achieved the stated aims of the institution's educational experience. Aims or outcomes are as varied as the mission and purpose of each institution. Most institutions are obligated to provide this evidence of students achievement to regional accrediting bodies and often to state educational agencies. Evidence is often provided as an aggregate picture of student achievement, but it also is used by individual colleges and departments to understand and reflect on the learning of their own students compared to institutional norms. Student affairs can and should participate in some of the assessment measures used by the institution by including a convenient cohort of students who specifically represent involvement in the cocurriculum. In the case of Texas A&M University, the cohort of involved students is represented by student leaders from across the Division of Student Affairs but primarily from residence life, student activities, the student center, student life (new student programs), Greek life, multicultural services, and recreational sports. Some of these students will have multiple leadership roles at the institution over time, but at the point they are asked to participate in the assessment, they are in a primary leadership role within a student organization.

A cohort of student leaders participating in institutional assessment programs can be a reason for applause and a cause for concern. Student leaders can outperform or underperform the institution's aggregate scores. Taking this approach to assessing student learning in the students' cocurricular leadership experiences requires the willingness to recognize when student leaders—irrespective of their major, college, or department—do not perform as well as other students who may or may not be involved. It also requires a willingness to take the results seriously and discuss, as a student affairs division, what might be done to increase student learning in the particular skill the survey program is assessing. Results that show students in the cocurriculum are performing at or above the institutional norm provide the academic community with evidence of learning and an affirmation for the work and commitment of the student affairs staff.

CAT (Critical Thinking Assessment Test)

In November 2008, Texas A&M participated in a pilot assessment of critical thinking skills among seniors across disciplines, using an instrument called the Critical Thinking Assessment Test (CAT). The instrument is a faculty-scored, one-hour, short-answer essay test designed to be interesting and engaging to students, with questions derived from real-world situations (Texas A&M University Core Curriculum Council, 2011).

The CAT instrument, designed at Tennessee Technological University and funded primarily by the National Science Foundation, is designed to assess students' mastery of a broad range of critical thinking and real-world problem-solving skills. It was developed with input from faculty from a variety of disciplines at six institutions across the country, who agreed that the following skills were the most important elements of critical thinking: evaluating information, creative thinking, learning and problem solving, and communicating ideas effectively (Tennessee Tech University, 2011).

In 2009–10, Texas A&M established a rotating three-year schedule shared among entities within the university's nine colleges and two branch campuses. Within each three-year period, each entity participates in the CAT once. In 2009–10, architecture, engineering, geosciences, science, and student affairs were the participants. On each of the four components of critical thinking, Texas A&M students outperformed the national norm on the CAT test. In addition, the average CAT score for student leaders from student affairs was greater than the average for Texas A&M (Office of Institutional Assessment, 2011).

Writing Assessment Project (WAP)

In collaboration with the University Writing Center, Texas A&M's Office of Institutional Assessment conducts a universitywide assessment of undergraduate student writing each year by analyzing hundreds of end-of-experience papers, scored twice by faculty using an established rubric (Texas A&M University Core Curriculum Council, 2011).

Texas A&M's general education outcomes for undergraduate students include communicating effectively and preparing to engage in lifelong learning. The WAP was developed to assess these learning outcomes. The WAP was piloted at Texas A&M during the 2008–09 academic year and continues to draw 400–500 papers from upper-level courses each year. Like the CAT, the WAP operates on a three-year rotating basis among the university's colleges and two branch campuses (Texas A&M University Core Curriculum Council, 2011).

As in the CAT, the Office of Institutional Assessment is open to having student leaders participate in the WAP as a cohort. The challenge for student affairs, however, is determining what written work student leaders would be asked to provide. Would student leaders be asked to prepare end-of-experience papers specifically for this project? Are there writing artifacts from the range of student leadership positions that would be comparable to papers in upper-level course work? Brainstorming possible student artifacts yielded a number of options: applications for scholarships, applications for leadership positions, reflection papers after service and volunteer activities, and annual reports and transition documents by leaders as they leave their positions.

Recently, several student affairs advisors, supervisors, midlevel managers, and department directors at Texas A&M discussed whether student leaders should participate in the WAP. The group was split. Many professionals in attendance recognized the valuable data that could be gathered from involvement in such an endeavor. However, others in the room noted that the writing style on a student leader application would most certainly differ from the writing style on an academic assignment. One staff member noted that, in fact, student writing *should* be different, depending on the context of the writing. For example, the style used to fill out an application for a resident advisor position differs from the style used to complete a paper for an upper-level literature class.

Following this discussion, the first fall 2011 professional development program for the Student Leader Learning Outcomes (SLLO) project was led by the director of the Texas A&M University Writing Center. The program's focus was on Texas A&M's undergraduate learning outcome to "communicate effectively, including the ability to demonstrate effective writing skills" (Texas A&M University Core Curriculum Council, 2011). The director provided information and resources about how to provide feedback to students on their e-mails, texts, sponsorship letters, reports, and more. She helped define what constitutes good cocurricular writing and gave a short refresher to advisors and supervisors about their own writing skills and assumptions about grammar and punctuation. She also indicated that the SLLO rubric on writing skills (see Appendices E and F in Chapter 5) was a good one to use to help give students feedback on their writing.

Considering the reservations about participating in the WAP, this developmental program with the University Writing Center's director suggested that an alternative to the WAP might be to use the SLLO writing rubric for an annual advisor review of student written work. For example, using the rubric and a predetermined scoring process, a group of advisors could score a variety of leadership applications from across the division for an aggregate view of student leader writing skills. This process could be used for a variety of evidence sources, including reflective papers or transition documents that student leaders prepare for their successors. Both the process and the rubric would need to be thoroughly researched and vetted by others in the university to ensure that this SLLO alternative for the cocurriculum would be comparable to and as respected as the WAP project.

Global Perspectives Inventory (GPI)

According to its website, "The Global Perspective Institute Inc. [GPI] was established in 2008 to study and promote global holistic human development, especially among college students" (GPI, 2011, para. 1). The GPI was developed to measure an individual's global perspective. The authors developed the GPI to measure three dimensions: cognitive, intrapersonal, and interpersonal. These three dimensions answer the following questions:

- "How do I know?" reflects the cognitive dimension. Cognitive development is centered on one's knowledge and understanding of what is true and important to know. It includes viewing knowledge and knowing with greater complexity and no longer relying on external authorities to have absolute truth.
- "Who am I?" reflects the intrapersonal dimension. Intrapersonal development focuses on one becoming more aware of and integrating one's personal values and self-identity into one's personhood.
- "How do I relate to others?" reflects the interpersonal dimension. Interpersonal development is centered on one's willingness to interact with persons with different social norms and cultural backgrounds, acceptance of others, and being comfortable when relating to others. (GPI, 2011, para. 3)

The GPI is a survey of 64 items, a few of which are biographical. Not only does it provide a self-report of an individual's perspectives in the cognitive, intrapersonal, and interpersonal dimensions of global learning, but it also records views on that individual's community and level of involvement in 12 curricular and cocurricular activities (Texas A&M University Core Curriculum Council, 2011).

Texas A&M implemented the GPI as a pilot in the 2010–11 academic year with random samples of freshmen and seniors and a comparison group of study abroad participants. The intention was that the GPI would provide evidence that demonstrated the attainment of the institution's undergraduate learning outcome that students will "demonstrate social, cultural, and global competence" (Office of Institutional Assessment, 2010). In the 2011–12 academic year, student leaders participated as a cohort in the GPI, and their aggregate scores were compared to the institution's aggregate score. Although the university involves both freshmen and seniors in the GPI, only senior student leaders were included from student affairs for the obvious reason that not many freshmen are in positions of student leadership yet.

Multi-Institutional Study of Leadership (MSL)

Until 2010, the Multi-Institutional Study of Leadership (MSL) was an annual, national survey of leadership development among college students. (Beginning with the 2012 administration year, the MSL will be administered every three years.) "It explores the role of higher education in developing leadership capacities with a special focus on specific environmental conditions that foster leadership development" (MSL, 2011).

The theoretical framework for the study was based on the Social Change Model of Leadership that has eight values: consciousness of self, congruence, commitment, collaboration, common purpose, controversy with civility, citizenship, and change for the common good (MSL, 2009). These dimensions intersect and interact on individual, group, and societal levels and lead to change for the common good (MSL, 2011).

Texas A&M administered the MSL in 2006 and 2009. In 2009, the survey comprised a random sample of 4,000 undergraduate students and a comparative sample of 500 students who were involved in student organizations, student employment, or student leadership experiences. Results indicated that 64% of the random sample and 69% of the comparative sample were applying what they learned in the classroom to their student involvement/leadership experiences. Sixty-six percent of the random sample and 79% of the comparative sample were applying what they were learning through their student involvement or leadership experience to their classroom learning (MSL, 2009).

At Texas A&M, the MSL is used to assess leadership development through participation in extracurricular activities as a first step toward developing leadership skills (Texas A&M University Core Curriculum Council, 2011). The University of Texas at Austin participates in the MSL as part of a comprehensive plan that assesses general student body leadership development and the effectiveness of specific leadership programming within the Division of Student Affairs (G. Stuart, personal communication, September 23, 2011).

National Survey of Student Engagement (NSSE)

NSSE annually collects information at four-year colleges and universities about student participation in programs and activities that promote personal learning and development. In 2010, 603 institutions participated; 1,452 institutions have participated since 2000. The results provide institutions with information about how their students spend their time and what they gain from attending their institution. Also, benchmark data is provided from the aggregate institutional results by individual question and by NSSE's five benchmarks of educational practice: level of academic challenge, active and collaborative learning, student-faculty interaction, enriching educational experiences, and supportive campus environment. In addition, students write in their intended major and secondary major, if applicable (NSSE, 2011).

The NSSE is administered to first-year and senior degree-seeking students. How often it is administered differs for every participating institution. Consistency of administration does help institutions develop longitudinal profiles of their students, from administration to administration and from freshman to senior year.

This is another opportunity to partner with entities on campus that conduct student learning assessment. As with the CAT and the GPI, the Division of Student Affairs is able to track the performance of student leaders in comparison to other students at the institution in terms of " . . . the time and effort they put into their studies and other educationally purposeful activities" (NSSE, 2011, para. 1).

Meta-assessment of Cocurricular Outcomes

The three institutions highlighted below shared their programs for gathering data to understand what students are learning in their cocurricular experiences: Vanderbilt University in Nashville, North Carolina; Weber State University in Ogden, Utah; and Northern Arizona University in Flagstaff, Arizona. All programs are in different stages of development. Vanderbilt University's Cocurricular Learning Initiative (CLI) is in the planning stage; Weber State University's plan was implemented in fall 2011; and Northern Arizona University has been working on its plan for several years. All show what is possible within the individual institutional context of mission, purpose, and student learning outcomes.

Vanderbilt University's Cocurricular Learning Initiative (CLI). The Vanderbilt CLI is based on the foundational definition that cocurricular learning is formal and informal learning that occurs outside the classroom. Critical characteristics that distinguish cocurricular learning are an intentional connection to learning outcomes, personal and professional development, and the integration of a self-reflective learning process that considers the holistic nature of growth and development (R. Jackson, personal communication, August 24, 2011)

The cornerstone of the CLI is assessing and mapping cocurricular opportunities for learning outcomes. This will allow students to make better-informed choices about their cocurricular involvement. When the technological infrastructure is completed, another primary benefit to students will be the ability to systematically track their cocurricular engagement, ultimately resulting in the creation of a cocurricular transcript.

The second principle component of the CLI will be its capacity to make training available and easily accessible for staff members, meeting the need for staff to be well informed of best practices for assessing and aligning program development to achieve desired learning outcomes. Also, CLI will increase students' capacity to distinguish the high impact value of various out-of-class experiences. To achieve the goal of increased knowledge about cocurricular learning and to assist in the training process, online modules will be developed for staff and students.

The third principle component of the CLI is the personal support option. Staff will be available to consult and serve as a central point for referral to existing resources. Although staff will primarily assist students, they will also help any other constituents interested in exploring, developing ideas, or connecting to cocurricular opportunities and collaborations.

The last component, but one of significant value, will be a community knowledge database. When fully functional, this will be a user-friendly web portal that provides 24/7 access for quick and easy exploration of out-of-class learning opportunities, resources, research, and articles on various topics relevant to cocurricular learning. The database will be organized by topics, key experiences, and interest areas.

Weber State University. Also beginning the journey of aggregating data about students' learning in the cocurricular is the Division of Student Affairs at Weber State University. According to Jessica Oyler, Coordinator of Student Affairs Assessment, the division has student learning outcomes that track to the institution's general education outcomes and the Association of American Colleges and Universities VALUE Rubrics. (Refer to Chapter 4 for more details on that project.) The Division of Student Affairs has developed a set of 7 to 10 survey questions for each of the division's outcome areas.

Departments will use the survey questions to indirectly measure student learning (J. Oyler, personal communication, June 23, 2011).

Weber State has also developed rubrics for each of its outcome areas and was to begin employing them in the fall of 2011. The intention is for a trained subcommittee of the division's assessment committee to use the rubrics to score student reflections and other writing exercises, while each department will choose one or two of the rubrics to use with observations and interviews. The next step will be to take the outcomes of each of these tools and aggregate them to the division level through the use of an online rubric tool. They also plan to aggregate the indirect survey questions around each of the outcome areas in the same way.

Northern Arizona University. At Northern Arizona University, the Division of Enrollment Management and Student Affairs does not aggregate the results of separate learning outcome assessments; but, like Weber State, it has a divisional survey. The process of developing the survey involved all 15 departments in the division. Representatives from all units were asked to identify learning outcomes for each of their key programs and activities—for a total of roughly 8 to 10 learning outcomes per department—and bring them to a meeting. From that meeting, a small work group was formed to identify common outcomes, eliminate redundancies, and whittle down the list of outcomes to be as inclusive as possible while maintaining a manageable size. Survey questions were developed from the selected outcomes.

Margot Saltonstall, assessment coordinator at NAU, noted the many challenges of combining learning outcomes data from individual programs to demonstrate student learning in meaningful and significant ways. Among the challenges she noted were collection of data at different points in time across the learning cycle and academic year, use of similar but not identical language/survey items that were to be combined, and duplicate responses that resulted when a single student completed more than one program's evaluation and those evaluation results were later combined. Thus, Saltonstall indicated the divisional survey has not only saved time and addressed methodological issues by eliminating the need to aggregate smaller data sets that did not align perfectly, but it also facilitated the development of a clear set of student learning outcomes for the division that underpins priorities across departments (M. Saltonstall, personal communication, June 21, 2011).

The survey is administered every fall to sophomores, juniors, and seniors. Prior to answering the 34 items concerning their self-reported learning outcomes on a 4-point scale from "not at all" to "very much," students are asked questions about their use of various services and participation in programs and activities. There are 5 additional questions with the same scale that ask students to indicate how their involvement outside the classroom in general has helped them prioritize the demands on their time, be successful academically, be successful in life in general, manage the stress or demands of college life, and manage their health and well-being. There are also two qualitative questions. The first asks students to describe any other activity that has significantly contributed to their college experience. The second asks them to provide other comments about being involved on campus and contributions to their learning and development that have not been addressed in the previous questions.

Data are analyzed in aggregate for a division-level perspective and disaggregated for particular outcomes that align with specific programs or services. Data can also be analyzed at the department level. Data analysis includes comparing users and nonusers of a given program/activity/service to the outcomes chosen by that program staff as most relevant. Data have also been used to compare the differences in responses between involved and uninvolved students.

Saltonstall noted that the data have been used in many ways and are presented frequently throughout campus. Often, results are included as one piece of assessment data for departmental strategic plan accomplishments. When combined with other evidence, data are used to set goals for maintaining or expanding a program where learning is occurring, as well as for changing efforts where learning does not appear to be occurring at desired levels. As a division, they report some of this evidence at new student orientation, in marketing materials, through roundtables, at their annual Assessment Fair, and eventually as part of their institutional reaffirmation for accreditation.

Basing Learning Activities on Student Development Theory

Self-authorship

Baxter Magolda (2008) began her study of self-authorship in 1986 when she interviewed 101 students who were beginning their studies at Miami University. Initially, she designed the study to explore gender differences based on the work of Perry (1970) and Belenky, Clinchy, Goldberger, and Tarule (1986). The study continued with 70 participants after college and with 30 who remained in her study by the 20th year. Continuing the study into the post-college years " . . . shifted the nature of the study to a more holistic view of self-authorship in young adult life" (p. 272). In 2004, Baxter Magolda and King defined self-authorship as:

The capacity to internally define a coherent belief system and identity that coordinates engagement in mutual relations with the larger world. This internal foundation yields the capacity to actively listen to multiple perspectives, critically interpret those perspectives in light of relevant evidence and the internal foundation, and make judgments accordingly. (p. xxii)

Baxter Magolda (2009) noted that figuring out our internal voice requires standing back from the external influences that shaped us as adolescents and deciding who we want to be and what our purpose in life will be. She insisted that developing our own internal voice helps us work through life's difficult challenges, helps us face unexpected circumstances beyond our control, and enables us to go forward with confidence. In effect, developing our internal voice shapes a foundation on which we can build our future. Here she described self-authorship as "using your internal voice and core personal values to guide your life" (p. 2).

Baxter Magolda (2009) described the developmental journey as starting from generally not being consciously aware of the rules that we use to describe ourselves and our life until we have an experience that contradicts them. For a time, we simply alter these rules to allow for what we consider exceptions to what we have always believed. We must pause from the journey and spend some time to reflect on and analyze these unexamined rules and decide what we think of them at this point in the journey. She explained that the part of the journey dependent on external formulas reaches a crossroads where we begin to listen to our own internal voice and then cultivate our internal voice to sort out our beliefs and establish our own priorities. The transition to self-authorship consists of learning to trust our internal voice to shape our reaction to reality that is beyond our control. The journey then turns to building an internal foundation or philosophy of life that will guide our actions. Finally, we secure internal commitments as we live them out daily.

Baxter Magolda (2009) reminded readers that the journey to self-authorship is complicated because there are multiple layers of development taking place at the same time. First, there is cognitive development, which means wrestling with what to believe and value as distinct from the beliefs and values formed by families, teachers, peers, and faith leaders. Second, we are working with intrapersonal development or coming to terms with how we view ourselves. In our adult lives, intrapersonal development can mean reshaping our identities to reflect our internal voice. And third, we are working on interpersonal development or how we want to interact with and build relationships with others.

Baxter Magolda and King (2004) believed that self-authorship should be a central goal of higher education. "Substantial evidence suggests that self-authorship is uncommon during college. Traditional age students rely heavily on external authorities and sources for their beliefs and values" (p. xxiii). Evidence suggests that students begin to recognize the need to compose their own realities when they are graduating from or after college. Specifically, Baxter Magolda (2009) suggested that desired college-level learning outcomes (critical thinking, developing identity and purpose, functioning interdependently) demand self-authorship rather than dependence on authority. She noted that her research showed that what kept her study participants reliant on external formulas was not their lack of capacity, but, rather, schooling and societal dynamics. Her participants' stories would indicate that they were neither challenged nor supported sufficiently to develop their internal voice sooner.

In the face of evidence that self-authorship can be developed in college, and because it supports desired college-level learning outcomes, Baxter Magolda (2008) insisted that " . . . because self-authorship is a capacity that allows young adults to better meet the challenges of adult life, enabling this capacity should be a key focus of a college education" (p. 282).

Self-authorship and Texas A&M University's Student Leader Learning Outcomes Project

After three years of commitment to intentional student leader learning and the development of many measurements to assess that learning (see Chapter 4), it became evident to advisors and administrators involved with the SLLO project that we needed to anchor our efforts in an overarching theory of student development and learning. The first effort in this regard produced a document called *SLLO: Self-authorship, Reflection, and Integrative Learning* (Osters, Roberts, Rodriguez, Scott, Wimberley, & Zuniga, 2011). The purpose of the document was to anchor the work of the SLLO project in Baxter Magolda's self-authorship model, establish the critical role of reflection in the process, and use both of these elements as the bridge to integration with students' academic journeys. At the time, however, those of us involved in the project knew much more about—and were more comfortable with—reflection and academic integration than self-authorship.

Previous assessments of the SLLO project goals have been designed without any grounding in scholarship. (Student learning based on the SLLO leadership skills rubrics are all based in scholarship.) The first effort was to assess the development of students in six organizations over a year, based on the use of rubrics. Three organizations were committed to using the SLLO assessment rubrics and three operated normally, without any personal learning agenda or assessment of their members. Both advisors and student leaders were surveyed three times during the year to determine if there were any differences among the two groups. In 2008–09, an assessment was conducted with advisors of student organizations to understand the challenges of embedding learning into a student organization's culture and the challenge that using the SLLO assessment tools presented. Also in 2008–09, student affairs organization advisors wrote reflective journals three times during the academic year. In the following year, student leaders of four organizations that had successfully integrated learning into their culture and used many of the SLLO assessment tools were interviewed. In all of these assessments, data were analyzed by a formal qualitative content analysis.

In 2008 when *SLLO: Self-authorship, Reflection, and Integrative Learning* was first shared with advisors, Osters et al. (2011) emphasized reflection as a way to produce small challenges in students' thinking about their leadership experiences. The authors provided a series of learning tools and questions for student leaders and executive groups to encourage introspection about their leadership experiences at various points along the journey, from the beginning to the end of the experience. The questions can be used with individual students and with an executive leadership team of a student organization. Responses can be given in a conversation format or through writing short answers.

In 2011, as members of the SLLO assessment working team began to understand self-authorship and the potential of the theory to inform and shape our work with students, we conducted a pilot project to determine how positional student leaders articulate their journeys to self-authorship. For purposes of this first pilot attempt, questions were shaped around students' perceptions of their integration of curricular and cocurricular learning, their strongest leadership skills, their greatest leadership achievement, their challenges to grow and stretch themselves as leaders, and the effect their experiences had on their values and beliefs.

Thirty-eight students (21 men and 17 women) who were exiting their leadership experiences or just beginning new ones in the spring 2011 semester were interviewed. The interviews were audio recorded. Twenty-five interviewers were trained in how to conduct the interview. The SLLO assessment working team developed a structured interview protocol in order to address the large number of interviewers and the relatively short time to properly train them. Interviews were scheduled for 60 minutes but actually varied from 20 to 60 minutes. These limitations—relatively untrained interviewers, structured interviews, and a short interview time—were contrary to the procedures that Baxter Magolda employed in her 21-year interviewing project and did not reflect the way she and King (2007) suggested that others could use interviewing strategies to assess self-authorship. These limitations have become some of the biggest lessons learned from the pilot project.

Despite these limitations, the 2011 pilot program offered some promising information. As of this writing, the data generated from the interviews are still undergoing a formal content analysis. Members of the SLLO assessment team, as well as other interested advisors who participated as interviewers, conducted the content analysis process and developed themes for each question. Two types of themes emerged: those that are the product of how 38 students answered each question and those that indicate the journeys of individual students toward self-authorship. Even though analysis and written reports are not yet completed, it is obvious that most students are anchored in environmentally determined values and beliefs and that only a few are at the crossroads of recognizing the need to develop their own internal voice.

Assessing a Student Learning Project

A student learning initiative is not undertaken in a vacuum. It is imperative to take a step back and consider how you will assess your progress toward encouraging, assessing, and documenting student learning. A project of this type deserves an assessment plan to keep you on track and thinking strategically.

As you are developing your plan, think about what you want the program to accomplish—not just what you want students to learn. What are your goals, outcomes, and measures? What does success look like? Those answers will drive the rest of the plan. If you are starting something from scratch, know that you can be flexible as the project matures and you try different initiatives.

Once you have an idea of the big picture, you can work down to more specifics. You may need to identify who has information that you need in order to determine if the program is successful and how you can improve. Obviously, students will have input, but advisors, supervisors, employers, the career center, faculty, supervisors of advisors, and student organization members can also provide feedback about their experiences. In addition, you could engage faculty in dialogue about student learning to strengthen the relationship and provide a seamless learning environment for students.

As you determine whom you might seek out, you can brainstorm what you want to know. Perhaps you want feedback from students about what it was like to learn in the cocurricular environment, how they have been able to use their intentional learning experiences when applying for jobs or internships, and what would engage their peers in the process. Chapter 5 talked about organizational development and change focusing on the staff member, but students may also be able to tell you how their student organization matured and their learning was reframed by the process. Career services or employers can give very valuable feedback about what skills student leaders/workers have developed over time and how to highlight this learning on their résumés. Staff may provide insight on challenges they faced, training they need, or changes they have witnessed when working with students in a group setting.

In addition, you have to consider in what form you want the information collected. Chapter 4 reviewed multiple assessment methods for data collection. As you are evaluating your program, methods such as interviews, focus groups, and surveys would easily work. Perhaps you conduct an electronic needs assessment for staff at the beginning of the year. If so, ask them to keep online or on-paper reflective journals for an academic year, and hold focus groups or interviews at the end of the school year or in the summer. Perhaps you could work with your career center to add a couple of questions to any employer survey already in place.

Because you could spend all your time collecting data rather than engaging in student learning, you have to think about reasonable timelines. *You do not have to assess everything all the time.* Create a plan that works for you. If you like the idea of focus groups with students, perhaps you could conduct them every other year or every three years. In the interim, you could plan to survey students about their learning or interview a selected group of student organization advisors. Many of the national surveys and tests can be expensive to implement every year, and they may not provide you with significantly different information from one year to the next. Depending on the length of the instrument, you could spend a year analyzing the data and making changes. What is important is having a well thought out plan that is manageable, forward thinking, and somewhat flexible.

Looking Ahead

This chapter provided a variety of strategies for assessing cocurricular learning on a macro-level. One method introduced cocurricular learning evidence through participation in institutional assessments with a cohort of involved students. Other methods were the Cocurricular Learning Initiative at Vanderbilt University; the use of rubrics at Weber State University; and an annual survey at Northern Arizona University that showcases the differences between involved and uninvolved students. The final strategy discussed was basing learning activities on a developmental theory such as Baxter Magolda's self-authorship model. All these methods have value and will be effective as they are a good fit with the mission and culture of individual higher education institutions and their student affairs divisions.

At Texas A&M University, with the continued development of the SLLO project, a number of these strategies will be combined to provide evidence of student learning in the cocurriculum. In particular, understanding the theory and assessment of self-authorship for student leaders will continue to be developed. In keeping with that goal, Baxter Magolda and King's (2004) Learning Partnerships Model will continue to be applied. As introduced in Chapter 5, Baxter Magolda and King described the delicate balance of providing guidance for students on their way to self-authorship and also being responsible for enabling the journey. They offered the Learning Partnerships Model as a means of blending the two to promote self-authorship. Society expects college graduates to manage complex environments and engage in multiple perspectives. Graduates are expected to act in ways that benefit themselves and others and contribute to the common good. Baxter Magolda and King described the model as follows:

> The Learning Partnerships Model introduces learners to these expectations by portraying learning as a complex process in which learners bring their own perspectives to bear on deciding what to believe and simultaneously share responsibility with others to construct knowledge. Because this vision of learning is a challenge to authority-dependent learners, the Learning Partnerships Model helps learners meet the challenge by validating their ability to learn, situating learning in learners' experience, and defining learning as a collaborative exchange of perspectives. (p. xviii)

Baxter Magolda and King (2004) believed that self-authorship should be a central goal of higher education and that the Leadership Partnerships Model can be a means of achieving that goal. They also asserted that educational partners are on the same journey. "Just as learners are learning to dance in the space between authority dependence and self-authorship, educators must learn to dance in the space between guidance and empowerment" (p. xxiii). As advisors working with student leaders at Texas A&M have discovered, guiding students in their leadership journeys also impacts one's own path of learning. Advisors have a new role. As Baxter Magolda and King said, "Creating partnerships through which learners engage in transformation from dependence on authority to self-authorship requires a corresponding transformation in educators" (p. 305).

Baxter Magolda (2009) suggested several ways in which educators can assist students in their journey toward self-authorship. She suggested using the six components of learning partnerships to promote students' inner voices and their ability to handle ambiguity. These components are comprised of three assumptions (knowledge is complex and socially constructed, self is central to knowledge construction, and authority and expertise are shared in the mutual construction of knowledge) and three principles (validating learners' capacity to know, situating learning in learners' experience, and mutually constructing meaning). The assumptions provide challenge and the principles provide support. Student affairs practice has been grounded in the theory of challenge and support since Sanford articulated the concept in 1967. The Learning Partnerships Model is a natural fit for students in their applied, cocurricular experiences and for student affairs staff.

The challenge will be to recognize that student affairs staff, especially newer professionals, may be working out their own inner voices. In fact, they may be on the journey *with* their students as well as *for* their students. This points again to the discussions in Chapter 5 about the necessary professional development needs of staff on the path of providing assessment for continuous improvement.

Questions for Reflection

1. Where is your division of student affairs on the journey of providing evidence of student learning in the cocurricular experience?
2. What direct measures of student learning (such as rubrics) could be used as evidence for cocurricular learning? Do these measures align with institutional goals and outcomes?
3. Do you have peers with whom you could collaborate to develop assessment tools that would allow you to benchmark against one another?
4. Do you have scholarship or a particular theory or model on which you base student learning in the cocurriculum?
5. What professional development will be necessary for staff to become partners with students on their learning journeys?

References

Baxter Magolda, M. B. (2008). Three elements of self-authorship. *Journal of College Student Development, 49*(4), 269–284.

Baxter Magolda, M. B. (2009). *Authoring your life: Developing an internal voice to navigate life's challenges.* Sterling, VA: Stylus Publishing.

Baxter Magolda, M. B., & King, P. M. (2004). *Learning partnerships: Theory and models of practice to educate for self-authorship.* Sterling, VA: Stylus Publishing.

Baxter Magolda, M. B., & King, P. M. (2007). Interview strategies for assessing self-authorship: Constructing conversations to assess meaning making. *Journal of College Student Development, 48*(5), 491–508.

Belenky, M., Clinchy, B. M., Goldberger N., & Tarule, J. (1986). *Women's ways of knowing: The development of self, voice, and mind.* New York, NY: Basic Books.

Global Perspectives Institute (GPI). (2011). Global perspective inventory. Retrieved from https://gpi.central.edu

Multi-Institutional Study of Leadership (MSL). (2009, Spring). Application of learning. Retrieved from http://studentactivities.tamu.edu/site_files/MSL%20one%20page--Application%20of%20Learning.pdf

Multi-Institutional Study of Leadership (MSL). (2011). Study description. Retrieved from http://www.leadershipstudy.net/ir-study-description.html

National Survey of Student Engagement (NSSE). (2011). About NSSE. Retrieved from http://nsse.iub.edu/html/about.cfm

Office of Institutional Assessment. (2010). *Texas A&M University general education outcomes assessment plan.* College Station, TX: Author.

Office of Institutional Assessment. (2011). *Critical thinking assessment test (CAT) institutional results: Texas A&M University, 2010–2011.* College Station, TX: Author.

Osters, S. N., Roberts, D. M., Rodriguez, V. D., Scott, M. L., Stone, R. L., Wimberley, L. A., & Zuniga, S. M. (2011). *Student leader learning outcomes (SLLO): Self-authorship, reflection, and integrative learning.* College Station, TX: Texas A&M University.

Perry, W. G. (1970). *Forms of intellectual and ethical development in the college years: A Scheme.* Troy, MO: Holt, Rinehart, & Winston.

Sanford, N. (1967). *Where colleges fail: A study of the student as a person.* San Francisco, CA: Jossey-Bass.

Tennessee Tech University. (2011). *Critical thinking assessment test.* Retrieved from http://www.tntech.edu/cat/home

Texas A&M University Core Curriculum Council. (2011). *2011 report of the Core Curriculum Council submitted to Texas Higher Education Coordinating Board.* College Station, TX: Author.

CHAPTER 8

OVERCOMING OBSTACLES AND MANAGING CHANGE

Darby M. Roberts

It seems we are, once again, provided with an excellent opportunity to think critically about the work that we do, how it can best meet the needs of today's students, and its relevance to the mission of higher education. This kind of introspection takes courage. (Dungy, 2011, p. 40)

Creating a student learning and assessment environment does not happen overnight, and it may even be a little painful to make a culture shift. At times, we see more obstacles than benefits. Getting the right people in the right place at the right time can be a challenge even in a stable environment. Money, time, politics, student issues, and other concerns can seem overwhelming. In today's higher education environment, change seems to be the only constant, but we need to take the time for important introspection about our contribution to higher education. In order to succeed, we must be able to adapt to and lead change, as uncomfortable as that may be.

Obstacles

Several obstacles, including both human and environmental factors, need to be addressed in the assessment of student learning outcomes. Previous chapters have addressed how supervisors, advisors, and administrators are involved in the student learning process. Yet, changing behavior can be a challenge. In addition, we know that fiscal resources, stakeholder expectations, time, and other factors intervene. There are several common responses to an initial request to assess student learning. Here are a few that you may have heard (or even said):

- "I just don't have time. I'm too busy doing my job." Many staff manage multiple priorities and tasks to provide programs and services, complete administrative processes, and respond to day-to-day issues.
- "I know in my heart students are learning. Why do I have to prove it?" Until fairly recently, advisors and supervisors have not been required to provide evidence of learning, even though they know it when they see it.
- "How can you really measure change and development in students? It is too difficult to quantify." Staff who have not been trained in a variety of assessment methods or who equate assessment with complicated research techniques struggle with the process.
- "I have never assessed this before and don't know how. I'm too old to learn." Most staff did not go into student affairs to do assessment, nor were they exposed to assessment in their graduate program.
- "Does anyone really care?" As with other initiatives, staff may not see the fruits of their labor or get feedback from others. Without accountability, real change fails.
- "This, too, shall pass. It's just a fad." Seasoned staff have seen multiple change efforts, some that flourished and some that failed. Different leaders proposed different initiatives. What should you support that will be meaningful, manageable, and a good investment of your time and energy?

How do you overcome these responses? As reviewed in Chapter 6, a supervisor or leader needs to set clear expectations and hold staff accountable. Quality assessment takes time, patience, and motivation. Some new staff do not have the training or experience, and some seasoned staff may also have a negative attitude about changing what they have successfully done for many years. However, new staff may have more education on learning outcomes assessment from their graduate programs, and older staff may have developed a comfortable and confident style working with students.

Financial Resources

In today's higher education environment, financial resources are a shrinking commodity. In a focus group of campus leaders, Kinzie (2010) found that "assessment is seen as resource intensive and—in the face of current budget crises on many campuses—by some leaders, as close to unsustainable" (p. 13). Creating a new project when many others are being cut seems counterintuitive. But developing a course of action that many people can align with to support the mission of the institution seems to make sense. So how do you implement something new on a limited budget? Critically examine what expected costs could be. Time and commitment are often more important than the actual money involved. Staff involved in the project take time to create methods to assess student learning, train their peers, and evaluate the success of the program on a regular basis. Nonetheless, having a small pot of money is helpful to pay for any printing, supplies, refreshments, professional development, or even a dedicated graduate assistant who can help move the project along.

Swing and Coogan (2010) explored the cost-benefit ratio of assessment, noting that the best option lies somewhere between doing too little meaningful assessment and too much assessment that overwhelms the institution's ability to process data and make substantive changes. In short, "while spending matters, it is equally important that the results gained yield a positive return on investment" (p. 6). Categories of cost to consider include instrument, administrative, human resources, and technology, although neither the cost of making improvements based on the data nor administrators' planning time would be included (Swing & Coogan, 2010). Some specific potential cost examples include survey and data analysis software, the salary for a graduate assistant to do the data analysis, paper/copying, professional development funding, and enrollment in national studies.

While some would argue that assessment is an expense, others say it is an investment. In financial terms, an expense delivers a short-term benefit, but an investment provides a long-term gain (Swing & Coogan, 2010). Collecting data and taking no action from it clearly is a cost without any offsetting benefit. In reflecting on earlier chapters that addressed institutional accountability, assessment might be seen as a cost: conducting assessment to satisfy accreditation requirements. Alternatively, the investment concept supports assessment for the improvement of student learning—a process that may never end.

The benefits of assessment may be more difficult to calculate concretely, especially if you are trying to do it for the student, the institution, and the greater society as a whole. However, institutions have become accustomed to estimating the value of a degree and calculating time to degree and retention rates. In a study of the relationship between higher education spending and student learning, Wellman (2010) concluded:

1. Intentionality matters as much as or more than money alone.
2. Focusing resources on instruction and student services helps increase learning, retention, and degree attainment.
3. Student financial aid programs need to be restructured to support the goal of student degree attainment as well as access.
4. Excess units and student attrition cost money and do not help students get to the finish line. (p. 16)

As student affairs professionals, we, too, have a responsibility to help students progress through our institutions in a timely and successful manner. Rather than using scarce resources as an excuse to avoid assessment, we should embrace the opportunity to learn more about how, when, where, and why students learn in our areas. There are many ways to initiate valid assessment on a small scale with few, if any, funds.

Marketing

How do you build basic knowledge and support for a new initiative? Particularly in larger or more decentralized organizations, marketing may be a necessary communication tool. Newsletters, presentations (internal and external to the organization), websites, social media, reports, and more provide information to multiple audiences. Of course, you need to identify your audiences as well as the message you want to convey in order to build your brand.

Your target audiences or market segments may be student organization advisors, supervisors of students, upper-level administration, students, and division staff. Each may require different communication. For example, in terms of message, you might be recruiting people to be part of the planning initiative, seeking people to attend training, or explaining how you are promoting the university learning outcomes. In terms of students, know what motivates them and what form of communication they prefer.

As you develop a plan, you have to articulate the benefits of participation before articulating the features (P. Busch, personal communication, September 22, 2011). Benefits answer the question, "What is in it for me?" For student organization advisors and supervisors, a question might also be, "What is in it for the students with whom I work?" Benefits may include access to resources, skill development, rewards for participation, a job/internship offer, or something else that motivates someone to engage in student learning assessment. The features of a marketing plan include the actual resources such as access to rubrics or learning contracts, an online assessment community, or a library of activities to encourage student learning.

The best piece of advice is to build collaboration. Who will be willing partners in assessing and documenting student learning? More minds will help clarify a direction to take to build support on your campus. Having a diverse group of early adopters can provide insight into building commitment from others.

Human Resources

For some large-scale environmental changes, leading from the middle can be an advantage and a disadvantage. Top-down changes are imposed by senior leadership. People may adopt the change because of hierarchy rather than a belief that the change is good for the organization. In many organizations, there are people with the ability to span the hierarchy regardless of title; including them in change processes may increase the chance for success. As Taylor (2007) described it, "Leaders are able to influence based on their personal power, which derives from many sources—expertise, experience, knowledge, reputation, position, and perhaps even personality" (p. 133). Leading change is about connecting people, ideas, and processes to accomplish a common goal. Taylor also said, "Effective leadership creates change, motivates and inspires others to act, aligns people with new realities, innovates, develops people for new roles and responsibilities, thinks strategically, challenges the status quo, and establishes a new direction" (p. 139). As you initiate student learning programs, keep in mind the stakeholders all around you, and keep them informed of your efforts, enlisting assistance when needed.

Time Management

How many student affairs professionals do you know with lots of free time on their hands? These days, with fewer resources, growing and shrinking enrollments depending on particular campus situations, smaller staffs, and greater expectations, student affairs professionals must balance their time and energy. Time is measured by semester or quarter. Some staff have busy times of the year; others have a more steady stream of activity. We spend hours in meetings, late nights with students, and weekends on retreats. Time seems to be the most valuable resource. Trying to sell staff on taking on "just one more thing" requires a carefully crafted plan that emphasizes the importance of change, their role in the change, and the benefits of that change.

Environment and Accountability

The current environment in higher education has focused on accountability, usually imposed by external organizations driven by shrinking funding sources. As Ekman and Pelletier (2008) noted, "An acrimonious debate has broken out in higher-education circles about institutional accountability and performance" (p. 15). That pressure can be imposed on student affairs. Alternatively, staff may truly believe that assessing student learning is important in itself.

Creating a culture of assessment of student learning takes a paradigm shift and a supportive environment. As Love and Estanek (2004) stated, "Assessment is too often seen as something being imposed from outside or from above, something at best tangential to student affairs work, which implies that to excise assessment practice would result in no overall loss for the organization" (p. 84). Although assessment in student affairs does happen because of external forces (e.g., accreditation, budget cuts), the best environment for assessment occurs when it is encouraged and expected at all levels of the department, division, and institution. In reality, upper levels of an organization may expect assessment, but it is usually new professionals and middle managers who make it happen. Consider bringing together experienced and new staff to work on a large project.

Institution Type

Each institution has its own unique personality, and the type of institution affects the mission and priorities related to learning outcomes assessment. Large research universities may have decentralized systems with a clear focus on faculty research and publication. Student learning is expected in the classroom; the out-of-class experience may be tangential. Small liberal arts institutions focus more on the whole student, and faculty and staff perform multiple functions. Faith-based institutions have a foundation of beliefs that may lead to a set of learning outcomes. Community colleges have their own challenges. Nunley, Bers, and Manning (2011) identified 11 of them, some of which overlap with 4-year institutions:

1. multiple missions of community colleges;
2. student characteristics;
3. absence of programs in baccalaureate degrees;
4. de facto program designation (lack of a clear completion path);

5. alternative learning venues;
6. limited professional support (especially in institutional research);
7. cost of assessment;
8. low faculty interest and engagement in assessment;
9. large number of adjunct faculty;
10. faculty collective bargaining agreements; and
11. community college governance.

To address those challenges, Nunley, Bers, and Manning (2011) provided several guidelines and cautions for community colleges. Once again, some of them could be translated to different institutional types. In brief, their guidelines encouraged institutions to

1. focus on the purpose;
2. create a meaningful process;
3. assess to learn;
4. be realistic about faculty involvement;
5. keep it simple;
6. supply professional and logistical support;
7. provide recurring professional development;
8. recognize that assessment data are at best one and only one source of evidence about institutional effectiveness in facilitating student success;
9. emphasize analysis and use of results above all else;
10. celebrate good work; and
11. acknowledge that assessment is messy, imperfect, and always incomplete.

Their cautions provided suggestions for making assessment manageable: Do not attempt a "one size fits all" model, do not select the assessment tool before determining the intended outcomes, do not let the administration or nonfaculty entities drive assessment, and be careful about making learning outcomes assessment one person's job (Nunley, Bers, & Manning, 2011).

Tradition and Culture

Klumpyan (2007) described tradition as "rooted deeply in organizational culture" (p. 95) and encompassing "the behavioral norms and values held by the organization" (p. 95). On the one hand, tradition provides identity, consistency, and stability. On the other hand, it can be an impediment to change ("We have always done it that way!"). Some student organizations rely on traditions and rituals to meet their mission and goals and create a unique experience for members. What would the campus look like if the tradition were one of a learning culture that all faculty, staff, and students supported and engaged in? Because learning is inherently a change process, the culture would be one of innovation and improvement. The consistency would be an acceptable level of change, not one that continually disrupts people's well-being, but one that nurtures development and knowledge.

Change

As Kuk, Banning, and Amey (2010) stated, "Adapting to change is an increasingly expected norm in organizations. In fact, change theorists hold that organizations must be designed to change if they are going to survive and be successful" (p. 25). People in those organizations need to be flexible, yet visionary. Many change theories exist, although few address the specifics of higher education and student affairs. Kuk, Banning, and Amey (2010) emphasized that different approaches, methods, and models exist to be adapted to unique organizational environments and cultures.

Kezar (2009) addressed some common challenges to and opportunities for change in higher education. One way to assist in change is to develop synergy. "If change agents and leaders made it a priority to better understand the multitude of initiatives already happening in their campuses and across the academy, they could consider a variety of options for creating greater synergy" (Kezar, 2009, p. 20). Building a cross-functional program from the bottom up creates a sense of ownership; leaders may not want to squelch the buy-in, but they also need to provide the means to connect the effort with others on the campus. Even within student affairs, we need to lower the number of silos and build structures that allow staff to come together around larger concepts—student learning, diversity, technology, assessment, etc. On larger campuses, staff may be duplicating efforts without even knowing it. Developing communication and planning structures can alleviate the waste of resources.

Once you, the unit, or the division identify the initiatives, it is necessary to decide the priorities for dedicating human and financial resources. The range of initiatives, politics, and timing on a college campus can make it difficult to set priorities (Kezar, 2009). To keep the process manageable, it may be helpful to get people to focus on a finite set of prioritized changes. In terms of student learning, staff are more likely to buy into the change effort if they are taught what it is, how to encourage it, and how to assess it. Once a core group of people has been identified, the professional development can begin (see Chapter 6 for more information about orientation, training, and continuous development). This may require that experts provide more training and support for staff than in the past.

Staff and leadership turnover can be a challenge and an opportunity. Often, "presidents and administrative leaders' terms in office are relatively short" (Kezar, 2009, p. 21), so it is difficult to sustain change efforts. New leaders come in and make their own set of changes. Therefore, student affairs department leadership may need to rely on staff who will be on campus for longer periods of time. Yet staff members who have been on campus for a long time may resist change efforts. New staff may come in with enthusiasm and theoretical knowledge, looking for a way to apply it, but they may lack the campus understanding of how and where to start the implementation. Bringing together new and old staff who have a variety of backgrounds and experiences creates opportunities for effective change.

Successful change takes planning and time for implementation. Chapter 6 explained one model of organizational change using eight steps (Kotter, 2006):

1. Establish a sense of urgency.
2. Form a powerful guiding coalition.
3. Create a vision.
4. Communicate the vision.
5. Empower others to act on the vision.
6. Plan for and create short-term wins.
7. Consolidate improvements and produce still more change.
8. Institutionalize new approaches. (p. 243)

These steps generate action and buy-in and are relevant to the higher education and student affairs environments.

Case Study Using Eight Steps of Organizational Change

The following case study highlights how the Student Leader Learning Outcomes (SLLO) project gained traction and support in the Division of Student Affairs at Texas A&M University. It required a paradigm shift, consistent attention, and commitment from a core group of staff.

1. Establish a Sense of Urgency

Within the institution, student learning outcomes assessment became a top priority. Although assessment was already gaining traction within the Division of Student Affairs, student learning was not at the forefront. Upper-level institutional assessment staff were bringing faculty and staff together to develop an assessment culture. The institution needed to develop a process to demonstrate assessment of student learning for accreditation purposes. Division leadership expected student affairs staff to be part of the learning mission of the university. In addition, the vice president of student affairs wanted to be able to talk to academic deans about the out-of-class experiences that benefited students in particular academic areas. Workshops were offered to faculty and staff on developing assessment plans, using rubrics as assessment measures, and following an assessment cycle. The student affairs assessment staff were challenged to motivate and train staff on student learning assessment.

2. Form a Powerful Guiding Coalition

The Department of Student Life Studies brought student organization advisors together to brainstorm the skills that students should gain from their leadership experiences. More than 30 skills were identified and categorized. Student Life Studies agreed to host the project because of the assessment component but also because the department did not have any ownership of student organizations, leadership training, or student programs. Several staff volunteered to be part of the guiding group to lay the foundation. Staff were mid-level professionals who performed well in their job functions, were respected within the division for their consistent performance, and had a personal interest and passion for student learning.

3. Create a Vision

Because of the institutional emphasis on student learning assessment, part of the vision was already created. A team of people developed a vision, mission, and goals that could relate to most of the staff in the division. The priorities set by the vice president for student affairs provided additional impetus from the top. Through training and conversations, staff began to see and embrace the importance of student learning.

4. Communicate the Vision

Every opportunity to talk about the student learning movement was utilized. The vice president was willing to promote it in discussions with directors. Staff involved were able to talk to their peers enthusiastically to gain momentum. A planning committee developed a training session and cast a wide net, inviting staff of all levels from across the division, including the vice president—who attended! Participants received a framed certificate to post in their offices.

5. *Empower Others to Act on the Vision*

You have probably heard the phrase, "People are committed to what they help create." From the very beginning, staff were encouraged to participate as they could. Work teams were created to develop student learning outcomes and associated rubrics. That gave staff autonomy and the opportunity to accomplish something tangible.

6. *Plan for and Create Short-term Wins*

As noted above, staff came together in work teams to develop learning outcomes and rubrics. For the staff who liked developing rubrics (and later learning contracts, leadership moments, etc.), this provided an opportunity for widespread participation, sometimes with a short time frame. Staff members have different crunch times throughout the year depending on their position; giving them the opportunity to participate at different times allowed them to be involved and feel valued.

7. *Consolidate Improvements and Produce Still More Change*

Because the project continued to change and develop, there was a great need for reinvigoration. Once the rubrics were created, the project hit a lull. One staff member decided that she would jump in and test one of the rubrics with the organization she advised. New training and development techniques were used. Rather than a three-hour session and monthly meetings, casual "coffee talks" led by staff were implemented. When that did not take off and feedback was gathered from advisors, meetings were restructured and a summer retreat was developed. When the idea of rubrics did not appeal to everyone, different assessment tools were used, so there could be something for everyone. The SLLO project also had to be re-branded to be more than rubrics. One of the major reasons the project was successful was the ability of the leadership team to create an environment that was fluid and adaptable. From the outset, the project took on an organic nature, meeting the changing needs of a dynamic and diverse division of student affairs. Team members also strove for excellence, not resting on their early successes but instead pushing themselves to create, assess, and re-create on an ongoing basis. In order to do this, the project's leadership team morphed with the project, adding members and skill sets when needed to accomplish the tasks at hand.

8. *Institutionalize New Approaches*

Many staff refer to "SLLO," although a few may not be up to date on the most recent developments. There are times it seems SLLO receives more attention from outside the institution. Marketing materials are taken to placement conferences to let potential candidates know that they can be involved in the project when they begin employment. The SLLO project leaders regularly present to staff, write newsletter articles, and seek feedback. The annual retreats consistently fill up, as do the semiannual orientation sessions.

Challenges to Change

Klumpyan (2007) offered four challenges to change and suggestions for responses. While meant specifically for mid-level managers, they provide discussion points for staff at all levels of the organization. Change Challenge #1 is "For what purpose?" (p. 88). People affected by the change should understand the need for it, the goals, and the expected long-term results. Otherwise, staff may resist, move in a different direction, or even sabotage the change efforts. To address the issue, Klumpyan emphasized the connection to purpose. To build trust in the process, she recommended explaining how the outcomes relate to a larger vision, mission, purpose, and goals. In addition, it is essential to seek commitment from upper administration and stakeholders and to create an effective communication plan.

Change Challenge #2, "What, not who, is going to drive the change?" (p. 90), emphasizes that people need to understand and support a cause, not just follow people who lead change. Klumpyan suggested creating an empowered team of champions who have varied skills and perspectives. The team should have a clear understanding of the purpose of the group and of individual contributions, create and agree upon a vision, and develop a process in which to work and communicate. Change should not be driven by personality, but rather by purpose.

Change Challenge #3 addresses communication. Have you ever felt like you are communicating, but no one is listening? Most problems can be solved through communication, and yet we still struggle with providing the right communication with the right people at the right time. In the absence of information, people tend to make up their own. To counteract this phenomenon, Klumpyan emphasized, "You cannot talk about change too often or too much" (p. 94). She summarized the team communication plan: Incorporate timelines, reconnect to the purpose, provide information in frequent small doses, create a unified front, develop a feedback process, and share short-term wins.

Klumpyan (2007) described Change Challenge #4 as "How do we get this change to become the norm?" (p. 95). She suggested being patient as the change becomes the norm, but in the meantime, reward people who are sustaining change, continue to communicate about the change, reconnect to the purpose, and institutionalize the change by integrating it into daily work.

In discussing the role of senior student affairs officers in innovation, Smith (2011) made the case that higher education changes have typically been externally motivated and particularly slow, but the current environment may in fact instigate change. He described innovation as the "bridge between creativity and change" (p. 226) and as the search for solutions through risk taking, creativity, and even failure. Although Smith focused specifically on the issue of attrition, his conclusions could be adapted to student learning: Vice presidents could "play a decisive role in stimulating success on campus by leading the efforts of innovation and change" (p. 229). Senior student affairs officers may not have the hands-on responsibility to assess student learning, but they set the expectations, hold staff accountable, and create an overall student learning culture.

Where Do We Go from Here?

You might be ready to initiate student learning assessment on your campus. Kuk, Banning, and Amey (2010) provided some insight:

> Some emergent factors that are important to consider as one begins to adapt and change in student affairs are senior administrative support; distributed leadership and ownership; transparent, inclusive processes built on the value of collaboration; a climate of planning and strategy development; organizational culture; and sufficient training, development, and institutional resources. (p. 147)

It is important to have a flexible plan, be able to predict consequences, and spend time building coalitions both up and down the hierarchy of the organization.

Iwata (2011) summarized Heifetz, Grashow, and Linsky (2009) in describing three tasks that leaders undertake to manage change:

- Fostering adaptation: Helping people develop their "next practices" to enable their organizations to thrive.
- Embracing disequilibrium: Keeping people in a state that creates enough dis-

comfort to induce essential changes in the workplace without creating despair, anger, or resignations.

- Generating leadership: Giving people at all levels of the organization the opportunity to experiment and lead, to facilitate your organization's capacity to adapt. (Iwata, 2011, p. 81)

Iwata (2011) concluded that, using the above parameters and maintaining emotional balance, the rewards of change outweigh the risks. The results lead to continuous improvement, adoption of best practices, staff commitment, and overcoming of obstacles.

You may be thinking, "That is all good in theory, but where do I go from here?" The simple answer, to borrow Nike's motto: Just Do It. Start where you can with small successes. The first step may be to have conversations with your colleagues about student learning and assessment. Build a core group of staff who are interested in moving down the student learning path. Invite people who are also interested in assessment; they may not have all the skills, but they should be interested in learning about multiple methods. The process can go in several directions but should include organizational learning related to assessment, student learning, and the institutional priorities. Some institutions and student affairs staffs may need to define their student learning outcomes, while others will just need to determine which ones they will focus on. Some institutions may have already developed assessment processes; others will need to seek out educational resources. Some institutional cultures already actively engage students in their learning; others have the opportunity to develop a process of student buy-in.

As discussed in previous chapters, the student learning effort and assessment may appear to be add-ons to already busy schedules, increasingly complex demands, and shrinking resources. Rather than focusing on the additional responsibilities, focus on how these things can be incorporated into your daily life. Realistically, the initial learning curve to improve skills will require time and energy, but rather quickly those things can be incorporated as part of the usual process. For example, to get students to start reflecting about their own learning, ask them about what they learned last week, rather than what they did last weekend. When planning programs, incorporate an assessment attitude from the very beginning—such as by asking "How will I know the program has been successful?"—rather than an afterthought (or no thought).

If assessment is not a natural part of your job yet, then be sure to start with something simple that will give you an easy win. What do you know you do well but haven't had the time to assess? What assessment method are you most comfortable with? How can you marry those two things in a way that is meaningful and manageable?

Conclusion

Although there are many challenges surrounding assessing and documenting student learning in the cocurriculum, there are as many reasons to engage in it. Resources, time, environment and culture, and fear of change all encourage the status quo. However, reasons for why we should be undertaking a change movement include the demands of accreditors and other stakeholders, the continual evolution of student affairs and higher education, and the students themselves. There is no better time to engage in the cocurricular learning process. It is not about the student affairs side of the house versus the academic affairs side of the house; students experience their learning as a holistic process. We should be active participants in that process.

You may be a senior student affairs officer, a middle manager, or a new professional working in a community college, a religiously affiliated institution, or a large research university. No matter your age, stage, or functional area, you can engage in assessment of student learning in support of the mission and outcomes of your institution. Student learning is everyone's responsibility.

Questions for Reflection

1. What barriers to change can you identify on your campus, thinking about all levels of the organization?
2. What skills do you have to lead change? Who else in your organization has skills to work on a team?
3. How can you gather resources on your campus to support assessment of student learning?

References

Dungy, G. J. (2011). Change is the only constant. *Leadership Exchange, 9*(2), 40.

Ekman, R., & Pelletier, S. (2008, July-August). Assessing student learning: A work in progress. *Change, 40*(4), 14–21.

Heifetz, R., Grashow, A., & Linsky, M. (2009, July-August). Leadership in a permanent crisis. *Harvard Business Review*, 62–69.

Iwata, J. M. (2011). The new nexus of transformational leadership in various collegiate settings. In G. J. Dungy & S. E. Ellis (Eds.), *Exceptional senior student affairs administrators' leadership: Strategies and competencies for success* (pp. 81–92). Washington, DC: National Association of Student Personnel Administrators.

Kezar, A. (2009, November/December). Change in higher education: Not enough or too much? *Change, 41*(6), 18–23.

Kinzie, J. (2010). *Perspectives from campus leaders on the current state of student learning outcomes assessment: NILOA focus group summary 2009–2010.* Urbana, IL: University of Illinois and Indiana University, National Institute for Learning Outcomes Assessment.

Klumpyan, T. (2007). Managing change from the middle: A translation for student affairs. In R. L. Ackerman (Ed.), *The mid-level manager in student affairs* (pp. 81–101). Washington, DC: National Association of Student Personnel Administrators.

Kotter, J. P. (2006). Leading change: Why transformation efforts fail. In J. V. Gallos (Ed.), *Organizational development* (1st ed., pp. 239–251). San Francisco, CA: Jossey-Bass.

Kuk, L., Banning, J. H., & Amey, M. J. (2010). *Positioning student affairs for sustainable change: Achieving organizational effectiveness through multiple perspectives.* Sterling, VA: Stylus.

Love, P. G., & Estanek, S. M. (2004). *Rethinking student affairs practice.* San Francisco, CA: Jossey-Bass.

Nunley, C., Bers, T., & Manning, T. (2011, July). *Learning outcomes assessment in community colleges* (NILOA Occasional Paper No. 10). Urbana, IL: University for Illinois and Indiana University, National Institute for Learning Outcomes Assessment.

Smith, L. N. (2011). The student affairs innovation imperative. In G. J. Dungy & S. E. Ellis (Eds.), *Exceptional senior student affairs administrators' leadership: Strategies and competencies for success* (pp. 219–231). Washington, DC: National Association of Student Personnel Administrators.

Swing, R. L., & Coogan, C. S. (2010, May). *Valuing assessment: Cost-benefit considerations* (NILOA Occasional Paper No. 5). Urbana, IL: University of Illinois and Indiana University, National Institute for Learning Outcomes Assessment.

Taylor, C. M. (2007). Leading from the middle. In R. L. Ackerman (Ed.), *The mid-level manager in student affairs* (pp. 127–153). Washington, DC: National Association of Student Personnel Administrators.

Wellman, J. V. (2010, January). *Connecting the dots between learning and resources* (NILOA Occasional Paper No. 3). Urbana, IL: University of Illinois and Indiana University, National Institute for Learning Outcomes Assessment.

CHAPTER 9

THE FUTURE OF STUDENT LEARNING IN STUDENT AFFAIRS

Kathy M. Collins

This chapter presents a preview of where assessment of student learning in the cocurricular environment is headed and how student affairs professionals can be engaged in the process. I will place special emphasis on the important role that the documentation of student learning in the cocurriculum plays in providing evidence of the effectiveness of experiential learning. In addition, I will explore the important role student affairs professionals can play in supporting the academic mission of an institution by providing evidence of student learning outside the classroom. Finally, I will examine the competencies and skills needed by current and future student affairs practitioners, who must strive to build a culture where assessing learning in the cocurriculum is commonplace. The future of higher education, student affairs, student learning, and professional development affects who we are as a society.

In summarizing the content of this book, I will first revisit the key concepts on which this book is based and review some of the important questions asked; then I will address the question of what is next in the assessment of student leadership in the cocurriculum. I will explore the key role that student affairs personnel play in documenting student leader learning outside the classroom, and I will review the competencies and skills student affairs staff need to do this work. Finally, I will examine the challenges student affairs staff face in higher education because of the aging education model and outdated learning tracking devices, and I will suggest new tools that will lead student affairs staff and our faculty partners into the future.

In Chapter 1, Dean Bresciani shared his perspective on the current environment of student affairs and higher education. He described the important role student affairs administrators play in providing students a quality university experience. During tough economic times, this role can be easily challenged when institutions are seeking to balance budgets and provide cost-effective options to students, family members, politicians, and other constituents.

Bresciani pointed out that, in the current economic environment, student affairs professionals must be strategic in their approach to their work and clearly articulate the contributions they make to the institution. No longer will student affairs be able to rely on passion and anecdotal evidence alone; it is time to provide hard evidence of the learning taking place in residence halls and through campus activities and student employee opportunities. Examining the results of isomorphism, it is easy to see that it, in the history of student affairs, has never been more important for our membership to acquire new skills and understanding to be able to clearly articulate and provide evidence of our role in student success and retention, revenue production, and lean operations.

It is the duty of everyone working in higher education to practice fiscal responsibility; however, it is the responsibility of the student affairs professional to run effective and efficient operations *and* continue to articulate his or her role and expertise regarding student learning to senior leadership, accreditors, and other challengers. The remaining chapters in this text highlighted a plethora of different tools available to student affairs professionals in articulating their role in student learning. Several authors emphasized how important it is for student affairs to document and provide evidence of student learning, in addition to assessing these practices with the aim of continuous improvement.

Whether the contributing author was a college president, vice president, or student organization advisor, they each touched on the importance of recognizing their role as educators. Everyone is responsible for fulfilling the role for which they were hired; everyone working in higher education is responsible for educating (Whitt, 2006). In Chapter 2, Sharra Durham Hynes wrote about the important role student affairs professionals play in preparing leaders to lead from the heart and true self. Building on this, in Chapter 3, Peggy Holzweiss described the importance for institutions to focus on student learning throughout campus. She highlighted a multitude of sources that are available to provide data on what students can learn in the college environment. It is important for student affairs professionals to embrace their role in the academy, in accreditation, etc. Perhaps most important, student affairs staff must carefully align the learning outcomes of their events/activities with the learning outcomes of the institution, as determined by the provost and senior leadership. Aligning outcomes from campus events and resident advisor training will build a student learning program that is seamless and supported throughout the campus.

Once student affairs professionals have created a culture of learning, staff will need to provide evidence that learning is taking place. The purpose of Chapter 4 was to review a variety of tools that can be used to effectively measure learning outcomes and track student learning in the cocurricular environment. Matt Starcke and Adrien DeLoach described how student affairs professionals could use rubrics, surveys, reflections, interviews and focus groups, portfolios, pre- and post-tests, and learning contracts to document the learning that is happening outside the classroom. The final phase of assessment involves students reflecting on their journey and recognizing the growth they have experienced through their involvement.

In Chapter 5, Katy King, described the student learning focused advisor as someone who supports holistic learning. She discussed the elements that indicate deep commitment to a learning institution and then examined the stages in the growth of a student organization and the accompanying evolution of the function of the advisor.

In Chapter 6, Krista Bailey said, "The student learning focused advisor and/ or supervisor is someone who values student learning, values the documentation of student learning, and actually documents the learning that occurs within the scope of his or her responsibilities" (p. 130). Bailey discussed the importance of creating a culture of learning supported by a framework of organizational culture. She wrote, "Organizations that are successful in supporting student learning not only promote the efforts but also have accountability measures in place to sustain the efforts" (p. 130). These organizations enhance the learning experience of their students and staff.

There are many strategies for creating a culture of learning, regardless of how the culture is addressed; student affairs staff must have a plan in place to assess cocurricular learning. In Chapter 7, Sandi Osters introduced the concept of participating in institutional assessments with a cohort of student leaders. She provided case study examples from Vanderbilt University, Weber State University, Northern Arizona University, the University of Texas, and Texas A&M University to showcase what institutions are currently doing across the country to foster a culture of learning on their campuses. Student affairs staff must be willing to make the time to conduct assessments on their programs, training, and more. Further, their practice of assessment must focus on the mission of the institution. This will place them in the perfect position to partner with students and faculty on their academic journey.

Student affairs staff have much to contribute toward the academic mission of an institution. However, our days, nights, and weekends are busy with meetings, programs, retreats, and training sessions. We even conduct hearings. Changing the way we do business will not be easy, but it is necessary. There is a fear of change, even among those who often consider themselves to be change agents. As Darby Roberts pointed out in Chapter 8, student affairs professionals are concerned about the amount of time that assessment will take and whether or not they have the needed resources, including human resources. Fortunately, senior administrators and even accreditors are demanding evidence that students are learning in the cocurricular environment. And, providing evidence of learning in campus activities, student unions, Greek life, and residence life is simply the right thing to do.

Where Assessment of Student Learning in the Cocurriculum Is Headed

The skills that matter for the 21st century are the ability to think creatively and to evaluate and analyze information (Silva, 2008). The idea that schools should focus on this type of student learning is nothing new. In fact, more than a century ago, American philosopher John Dewey argued for a system of education that taught more than just core academic subjects and instead taught students how to think. This call has intensified over the years, culminating in a 2006 report written by business leaders, governors, school leaders, and former secretaries of labor and education stating that basic skills are necessary but not sufficient in a world with a constantly shifting job market (National Center on Education and the Economy, 2006). Most important and often overlooked is the ever-present testing that our students are subject to—testing that is often standardized and more often than not requires nothing more than memorization and very little application of knowledge. Faculty and staff need to work together to develop better tools that measure the skills students need to succeed in today's world. These tools can be administered by both faculty and student affairs staff as we focus on the whole student and capture their entire college learning experience.

Today's students and many entry-level student affairs staff have grown up in a world overflowing with technology. Unlike many older faculty and senior student affairs practitioners, they do not have to adjust to new technologies; they simply adapt what they know about Blackboard, iPads, and their mobile phone to determine how to work a new device. Unfortunately, the few times in a year when students and staff are forced to unplug are often occasioned by antiquated higher education testing and tracking systems. Tools such as bubble sheets that must be scanned, blue books that need to be written in, training forms that must be signed, and rubrics and learning contracts that need to be completed on paper can dull a student's interest in their learning process. Advancements in assessment technology can answer many of these concerns. A student affairs partnership with information technology staff is paramount for delivering a successful learning experience to today's students. It is important to approach your partnership with information technology staff knowing that the technology and available gadgets should not drive the business process. Instead, the work that needs to be done to document student learning and run your daily operations should drive the technology. The focus needs to remain on student learning and the university's mission.

Developing superior assessment technology is only one of the ways in which higher education can deliver enhanced learning to students. Even more important is preparing and supporting quality student affairs professionals who can work with students and faculty to advance student learning in the academy. Student affairs professionals must find a way to be part of the student learning process. One way to do this is to provide evidence that the activities and employment offered throughout student affairs are laboratories where learning outside the classroom can take place. Our commitment to lifelong learning affects students' commitment to lifelong learning.

How Student Affairs Professionals Can Be Engaged in the Process

A gradual paradigm shift has been taking place on college campuses across the United States that will shape the role of the student affairs professional. The shift is transforming our campuses from places where instruction takes place to institutions focused on learning (Barr & Tagg, 1995). This new Learning Paradigm, so named by Barr and Tagg (1995), refocuses the mission of higher education from instruction to the production of learning "with every student by whatever means work best" (p. 1). Furthermore, this new paradigm places the institution itself in the role of learner. "A college is an institution that exists to produce learning" (Barr & Tagg, p. 1). For many student affairs professionals, student learning has always been a keystone to our work with students. However, as mentioned throughout the earlier chapters of this book, student affairs professionals have lacked formal means to document cocurricular learning, relying instead on anecdotal notions and student-requested reference letters to tell the story of the learning taking place through involvement in campus activities.

Today, in higher education in general, more (and louder) voices call for external accountability. As institutions as a whole respond to those calls, student affairs professionals should be paying attention to the issues as well. Ewell (2009) offered four principles to address the current tension. First, we are encouraged to "respond visibly to domains of legitimate external concern" (p. 14). This entails moving beyond publishing graduation rates to providing solid evidence of achievement in institutional learning outcomes, such as critical thinking and written communication. Being proactive shows a commitment to our responsibility in student learning. Ewell's second principle is to "show action on the results of assessment" (p. 15). It is not enough just to assess; the expectation is that something is done, based on assessment, to improve student learning throughout the institution. Not only should learning goals and outcomes be created, but all faculty, staff, and students should know them. Third, we should "emphasize assessment at the major transition points in a college career" (p. 17), including assessment prior to college, during the experience, and readiness to leave. Ewell's final principle is to "embed assessment in the regular curriculum" (p. 19), rather than in preparation for accreditation.

As student affairs professionals, we have always wanted our students and staff to learn and succeed. However, we have lacked the necessary tools to integrate our passion, our knowledge about learning, and our growing responsibility to provide documentation of learning for university partners and accreditation agencies. In the Learning Paradigm (Barr & Tagg, 1995), colleges take "responsibility for learning" and "a college's purpose is not to transfer knowledge but to create environments and experiences that bring students to discover and construct knowledge for themselves, to make students members of communities of learners that make discoveries and solve problems" (Barr & Tagg, 1995, p. 2). Most important, in this paradigm, institutions are not limited to only one means of instruction. Instead, campuses are encouraged to embrace a range of learning environments. Quality learning can take place in the classroom, but it can also take place in the student union, recreation center, residence hall, and on the intramural fields. Of course, tools are needed to document student learning outside the classroom, and this book has served as an introduction to many of the tools available to provide both direct and indirect evidence of learning in the cocurricular environment.

From their survey of provosts, Kuh and Ikenberry (2009) formulated recommendations for academic leaders, governing boards, faculty, institutional researchers, prospective students, parents, higher education associations, accreditors, and foundations. They also gave guidance to student affairs professionals:

Student affairs staff must share their perspectives on the student experience by participating on the campus assessment committee and self-study committees. Partner with academic affairs to promote a deeper, more widespread awareness and understanding of common undergraduate learning outcomes among faculty, staff, and students. Use outcomes assessment results to orient and inform student affairs practice. (p. 29)

Student affairs staff need to initiate action related to assessment of learning outcomes. Failure to do so could eventually result in elimination of staff, departments, or divisions of student affairs as described in Chapter 1.

Academic institutions have provided direct evidence of student learning for years. Direct evidence is tangible, visible, and self-explanatory evidence of what students have and have not learned (Suskie, 2009). Direct evidence comes in the shape of ratings students receive for their field experiences in student teaching, internships, and practicum (Suskie, 2009). Depending on a student's major, direct evidence can come in the form of a grade on a capstone experience or a research project, a thesis, a comprehensive examination, a dissertation defense, or a musical performance. Finally, and most closely related to the work of the student affairs professional, students' reflections on their values, attitudes, and beliefs are all forms of direct measures of learning.

Indirect evidence tells us that students are probably learning, but it is less convincing than direct measures of learning. Examples of indirect evidence include "course grades, assignment grades, retention and graduation rates . . . placement rates, alumni perception of satisfaction, student self-ratings of knowledge and skills . . . student, alumni, and employer satisfaction with learning . . . and honors, awards, and scholarships" (Suskie, 2009, p. 21). If you are unable to use direct measures, using multiple indirect measures is helpful.

In a university setting where the student affairs division is focused on learning, staff members are taught about the importance of constructing learning outcomes for everything, from individual sessions at resident advisor training to student organization retreats. A learning outcome is the knowledge, skill, or attitude that a student will gain from a learning experience (Suskie, 2009). Staff in student affairs must create student learning outcomes that are connected to the mission of the institution at which they are employed.

In a student affairs division focused on student learning, staff members not only know how to write learning outcomes, they are encouraged and required by supervisors and mentors to create appropriate opportunities for students to learn through involvement in cocurricular activities. More important, staff members are required to provide documentation of student learning through the use of rubrics, learning contracts, reflective journals, photography, and more. Furthermore, in a learning focused student affairs division, staff throughout the organizational chart are held accountable for student learning through expectations and through the formal university evaluation processes.

The division devoted to student learning will collaborate to recruit and select staff from student affairs master's programs that include assessment classes in their curriculum and graduate assistantships focused on student learning. These new personnel can bring their student learning experience from a variety of institutions and join your staff, creating a best practice scenario for student learning. Whether new ideas to enhance student learning on your campus come from a new hire, a peer institution, or a program sponsored by the Student Leadership Programs Knowledge Community in the National Association of Student Personnel Administrators, the important point is that student learning is taking place and you and your colleagues recognize that it is everyone's responsibility.

Like all assessment, providing evidence of student learning in the cocurriculum must become part of our everyday processes. Important decisions will be made based on the evidence we provide, and that information, as highlighted in Chapter 3, may become an integral part of your institution's accreditation report. Having student learning evidence readily available will assist you in making everyday decisions and long-range plans. As Bresciani notes in Chapter 1, this data will also speed up your decision-making processes and assist you in making effective budget and programming decisions. As this book stresses repeatedly, we have a responsibility to document student learning. We also have a responsibility to create a dynamic student affairs environment that has competent staff in the right positions.

As we move forward, we can learn from the experiences of others. As the Wabash Study progressed, Blaich and Wise (2011) translated their lessons learned into several steps to help others in their effort to enhance student learning:

1. Perform thorough audits of useful information that your institution has already collected about student learning and experience.
2. Set aside resources for faculty, student, and staff responses to the assessment information before assessment evidence is distributed across campus.
3. Develop careful communication plans so that a wide range of campus representatives have an opportunity to engage in discussions about the data.
4. Use these conversations to identify one, or at most two, outcomes on which to focus improvement efforts.

5. Be sure to engage students in helping you make sense of and form responses to assessment evidence.

As institutions and divisions of student affairs move forward with assessing and documenting student learning, these steps can help organize and frame efforts into manageable and important pieces.

Competencies of Students and Student Affairs Professionals

The competencies students develop through participation in campus activities can be highlighted in a résumé, but only if they provide evidence on that document of their campus involvement and their *learning*. When creating their résumé, most college students simply throw together a chronological list of leadership experiences; few student leaders will spotlight their learning and responsibilities. Student affairs professionals are aware that, depending on the campus, students will engage in a variety of roles during their tenure. Imagine the students who will oversee Texas A&M University's Fish Camp, an annual event that welcomes more than 5,000 students to campus and has an annual budget of more than $1 million dollars (Texas A&M University, Fish Camp, 2011). Or the students responsible for the oversight of Bowling Green State University's Dance Marathon, a yearlong event featuring more than 55 student organizations that culminates in a 32-hour dance marathon that, in 15 years, has raised more than $2 million dollars for Children's Miracle Network (Bowling Green State University, n.d.). The student leaders who direct these events certainly exercise critical thinking, project management, fiscal responsibility, delegation, and other competencies, skills closely aligned with their institution's stated learning outcomes for their graduates.

Like our students, student affairs staff should also be documenting their learning, updating their résumés and vitas, and tracking the development of their competencies. In 2010, a joint commission of the American College Personnel Association (ACPA) and NASPA released a document outlining the competencies expected of student affairs professionals. This document creates a road map for those of us who supervise middle managers and entry-level professionals. It is a map to skill development in the field. One of the competencies is assessment, evaluation, and research (ACPA & NASPA, Joint Task Force on Professional Competencies and Standards, 2010), the skill set that is the focus of this text. In the competency area of assessment, the advanced level includes the following abilities:

- Effectively lead the conceptualization and design of ongoing, systematic, high-quality, data-based strategies at the institutional, divisional, and/or unitwide level to evaluate and assess learning, programs, services, and personnel.
- Effectively use assessment and evaluation results in determining the institution's, the division's, or the unit's accomplishment of its missions and goals, reallocation of resources, and advocacy for more resources. (ACPA & NASPA, Joint Task Force on Professional Competencies and Standards, 2010, p. 11)

Clearly, it is the responsibility of student affairs professionals to understand and practice assessment, track student learning, track our own learning, and serve as catalysts for learning across campus. However, as discussed earlier, assessment has moved beyond bubble sheets and blue books. Our students have moved beyond rubrics and learning contracts on paper. They are demanding that we catch up to their technologically advanced world and create web applications and mobile and tablet applications that seamlessly track student learning from the moment students accept admission into our institutions. What we need is a software system that tracks a student's campus activity involvement and leadership development through online rubrics, learning contracts, mobile applications, and other tools.

What Is Needed?

The student affairs profession needs technology to support its assessment of student learning. Currently, depending on the campus, multiple databases and various documents are used for tracking student involvement. As a primary database, a campus may use a commercial or homegrown system; however, in student activities, it is likely that students are still applying for leadership positions using pen and paper. In addition, the same students may be completing paper forms or perhaps going to a website to apply for resident advisor positions, leadership scholarships, etc. The databases and forms used to track students' progress do not speak to one another, creating silos on even the smallest of our campuses. This way of doing business is as archaic as a residence life model that still uses pagers. Both leave a negative impression on a technologically advanced student body. It is time for an enhanced, web-based database, one that would track a student from the time of admission through commencement (and perhaps beyond). The database would be designed from the beginning for smart phones and tablets. The system would be the place where *all* students on campus would go to apply for student leadership positions and student employment opportunities. Students would only need to enter their information once, since the database is a secure repository of their time on campus. The database would track a student's achievements, building an electronic cocurricular transcript as the student moves successfully toward graduation.

Student organization leaders would use this technologically advanced system to create applications for their group's leadership positions, and student affairs departments and others would use it for student employment applications. Most important, students would use the system as a repository for their experiences and their own reflections. Finally, students would use the system as a means to communicate with potential employers. When the time came for students to apply for internships, cooperatives, and full-time employment, students would give access to certain parts of the database, allowing recruiters to view relevant information in the system that would highlight their accomplishments. Students could spotlight awards, titled positions, videos of themselves in action, and evidence of their student leadership work (budgets, agendas, etc.). Students and staff would love the ease of using one central database, and the system would bring the campus together—one campus, one system, focused on student learning.

Conclusion

This book brought together a group of authors with a variety of backgrounds who are all focused on student learning. The common thread running through their writings is the fact that it is the responsibility of everyone on a college campus to be involved in student learning. Higher education is a complex environment where change is the norm. Student affairs staff must break out of their silos and concentrate on building adaptable, sustainable practices that focus on the development of students and staff. Learning is certainly not a sprint. Learning is a long run, a slow jog, and a walk that will allow you to meet a wide variety of students, faculty, and staff. Learning is not easy, and it is perhaps our own learning that is the most difficult as we may be fearful of change and of approaches to our work that are unfamiliar to us. Yet, by simply reading this book, you are positioning yourself to better embrace new ways of practicing student affairs. Most importantly, you are ready to enhance the campuses on which you work by placing student learning at the center of the work you do with your students and colleagues across the campus.

References

American College Personnel Association (ACPA) & National Association of Student Personnel Administrators (NASPA), Joint Task Force on Professional Competencies and Standards. (2010). *ACPA/NASPA Professional Competency Areas for Student Affairs Practitioners.* Retrieved from http://www.naspa.org/programs/prodev/Professional_Competencies.pdf

Barr, R. B., & Tagg, J. (1995). From teaching to learning: A new paradigm for undergraduate education. *Change, 27*(2), 1–10.

Blaich, C. F., & Wise, K. S. (2011, January). *From gathering to using assessment results: Lessons from the Wabash National Study* (NILOA Occasional Paper No. 8). Urbana, IL: University of Illinois and Indiana University, National Institute for Learning Outcomes Assessment.

Bowling Green State University. (n.d.). Dance marathon. Retrieved February 6, 2012 from http://www.bgsu.edu/offices/sa/firstyear/connections/page76391.html

Ewell, P. (2009, November). *Assessment, accountability, and improvement: Revisiting the tension* (NILOA Occasional Paper No.1). Urbana, IL: University of Illinois and Indiana University, National Institute for Learning Outcomes Assessment.

Kuh, G., & Ikenberry, S. (2009). *More than you think, less than we need: Learning outcomes assessment in American Higher Education.* Urbana, IL: University of Illinois and Indiana University, National Institute for Learning Outcomes Assessment.

Middaugh, M. (2010). *Planning and assessment in higher education: Demonstrating institutional effectiveness.* San Francisco, CA: Jossey-Bass.

National Center on Education and the Economy. (2006). *Tough choices or tough times: The report of the New Commission on the Skills of the American Workforce.* San Francisco, CA: Jossey-Bass.

Silva, E. (2008). *Measuring skills for the 21st century.* Washington, DC: Education Sector.

Suskie, L. (2009). *Assessing student learning: A common sense approach* (2nd ed.). San Francisco, CA: Jossey-Bass.

Whitt, E. J. (2006, January-February). Are all of your educators educating? *About Campus, 10*(6), 2–9.

THE AUTHORS

Krista Jorge Bailey is an associate director in the Offices of the Dean of Student Life at Texas A&M University. Previous to that role, she was an associate director in student activities at Texas A&M where she was a founder of the Student Leader Learning Outcomes Project. During her career, she has advised many complex student organizations and events. She holds a doctorate degree in educational human resource development, a master's degree in educational administration, and a bachelor's degree in biomedical science and agricultural development, all from Texas A&M.

Dean Bresciani is the 14th president of North Dakota State University. Prior to assuming that position, he was the vice president for student affairs and a professor of educational administration at Texas A&M University. He has worked at a variety of institutions in various leadership and faculty roles in his 30 years in higher education. He holds a doctorate degree in higher education finance with a doctoral minor in economics from the University of Arizona, complemented by a master of education in college student personnel from Bowling Green State University; he received a BA in sociology from Humboldt State University.

D. Stanley Carpenter is the dean of the College of Education at Texas State University–San Marcos. He has held administrative positions including professor and chair of the Counseling, Leadership, Adult Education, and School Psychology Department at Texas State; dean of students at the University of Arkansas at Monticello; and executive director of the Association for the Study of Higher Education. In 2010, NASPA named him a Pillar of the Profession. His doctorate is in counseling and student personnel services from the University of Georgia. He holds a master's degree in student personnel and guidance at Texas A&M University–Commerce and a bachelor's degree in mathematics from Tarleton State University.

Kathy M. Collins is the director of campus living services and residence life at Michigan State University. Previous to that role, she was associate director of residence life at Texas A&M University. She has worked in student affairs since 1994, working in athletics, conduct, orientation, student activities, and residence life. She taught in the student affairs graduate program at Texas A&M and was a founder of the Student

Leader Learning Outcomes Project. She earned a doctorate degree in higher education administration from Bowling Green State University, a master's degree in counseling with an emphasis in college student personnel administration from Shippensburg University, and a bachelor's degree in political science/international relations–business from Juniata College.

Adrien DeLoach is an associate director for diversity education and training in the Office for Diversity and Inclusion at Virginia Polytechnic Institute and State University. Before assuming that position, he served as director of the Center for Diversity and Inclusion at Radford University and program advisor in the Department of Multicultural Services at Texas A&M University. He earned a master's degree in education, counseling, and student affairs from Western Kentucky University and is currently pursuing a doctorate degree in higher education.

Peggy C. Holzweiss is the assistant director of the Scowcroft Institute of International Affairs at Texas A&M University. She holds a PhD in higher education administration, an MS in student affairs administration, and a BS in psychology, all from Texas A&M University. She has experience in a variety of administrative areas including assessment, campus activities, student government, traditions, and residence life. She teaches in the student affairs graduate program at Texas A&M and was a founder of the Student Leader Learning Outcomes Project.

Sharra Durham Hynes is the vice president for student life at Houghton College. Prior to that position, she was associate director of student activities at Texas A&M University, where she was a founder of the Student Leader Learning Outcomes Project. In her 17 years of higher education experience, she has worked at a variety of institutions in administration, strategic planning, program design, and student learning and involvement. She holds a PhD in higher education administration from Texas A&M University and an MS in education in college student development from Alfred University.

Katy King is a program coordinator in the Memorial Student Center at Texas A&M University. In this role, she advises student organizations that conduct campuswide programming and supervises other advisors. She was a founder of the Student Leader Learning Outcomes Project at Texas A&M University. She holds a master's degree in educational administration and a bachelor's degree in marketing, both from Texas A&M.

Sandi Osters is the director of student life studies at Texas A&M University. Prior to that position, she was assistant to the vice president of student affairs. She has worked in judicial affairs, student activities, and residence life. She teaches in the student affairs graduate program at Texas A&M and was a founder of the Student Leader Learning Outcomes Project. Sandi holds a PhD in higher education administration from Texas A&M University; an MA in education, student affairs administration from The Ohio State University; and a BA in political science from Miami University.

Darby M. Roberts is the associate director of student life studies at Texas A&M University. She has worked in assessment since 1998. She previously worked in residence life and has advised student organizations for more than 20 years. A leader within the NASPA community, she served as editor of the Assessment column for *NetResults* magazine and is actively involved in the Assessment, Evaluation, and Research Knowledge Community. She teaches in the student affairs graduate program at Texas A&M and was a founder of the Student Leader Learning Outcomes Project. She holds a doctorate degree in educational administration, a master's degree in human resources management, and a bachelor's degree in business analysis, all from Texas A&M University.

Matt Starcke is the program coordinator for leadership and service in the Department of Student Activities at Texas A&M University. He has extensive experience in leadership and service programming and has advised a variety of student organizations at several institutions. He earned a master's degree in higher education administration from Texas A&M University and bachelor's degrees in English and economics from Southern Oregon University.